IRISH TELEVISION DRAMA

BROADCASTING AND IRISH SOCIETY SERIES

Edited by Richard Pine

The continuing story of Irish television drama

Tracking the tiger

Helena Sheehan

FOUR COURTS PRESS

Set in 10 on 13 point Janson Text by
Mac Style Ltd, Scarborough, N. Yorkshire for
FOUR COURTS PRESS LTD
7 Malpas Street, Dublin 8, Ireland
e-mail: info@four-courts-press.ie
and in North America
FOUR COURTS PRESS
c/o ISBS, 920 N.E. 58th Avenue, Suite 300, Portland, OR 97213.

A catalogue record for this title
is available from the British Library.

ISBN 1-85182-688-2 hbk
ISBN 1-85182-689-0 pbk

Printed in Great Britain
by MPG Books, Bodmin, Cornwall.

Contents

Illustrations

CREDITS

All illustrations © RTÉ Archive/Stills collection except 14 photograph ©
Patrick Dowling; 16 © Hat Trick Productions; 18 © Accomplice Television
Ltd; 19, 20, 26 photograph © Patrick Redmond and 21 photograph ©
Bernard Walsh.

Foreword

In 1986, one of my first major tasks as a member of the RTÉ Public Affairs Division was to see through the press the first edition of this book, Helena Sheehan's *Irish Television Drama: A Society and Its Stories* which RTÉ published the following year. The research for that book had been supported by Bob Collins, who was then Controller of Television Programmes. When, therefore, Bob Collins, as Director-General, asked me to edit a series of studies of RTÉ's programming, in celebration of its seventy-fifth anniversary, my thoughts immediately turned to Helena Sheehan's ground-breaking study of the dramatic genre as it had taken its place, and had been transmitted, on Irish television, and the writing of a sequel.

I recall being struck at the time by the intellectual vigour with which Dr Sheehan had pursued her research and her subsequent findings on the portrayal of Irish society in its television drama. I was even more impressed by the theoretical apparatus which she brought to bear, and which made the first edition of this book such a valuable introduction to the subject, for what has proved to be several generations of students. It is therefore a matter of deep gratification that the first edition of *Irish Television Drama* has been re-issued with this new volume, in the form of a CD-ROM.

Whether one agrees or disagrees with Dr Sheehan's analysis of RTÉ's drama output since 1962 – and much of it challenges the reader in ways that are disturbing and unconventional – one cannot fail to be impressed by the conviction and commitment which shines through her determination to convince her readership of the necessity of bringing the highest standards to the closest examination of what Ireland's storytellers are attempting to achieve on the television screen. Not everything on that screen which falls into the category of drama is meant to be world-shaping or even serious, and a series such as *The Irish RM* probably does not deserve the criticism she levels at it; nevertheless, when Dr Sheehan speaks of the 'passive and unreflective nature of much television viewing' and the 'shallow and fragmented character of most television criticism' she strikes a more than familiar chord and reminds us that drama is one of the most potent ways of asking people to reflect on their society, one that demands that we pay due attention to what is being said and, too often, what is not being said. Her constant appeal to her readers to make those examinations is a necessary reminder that we can all too easily dismiss, as casual, media representations that can inform, and determine, the courses of our own lives and our relations with others, either domestically or on the broader political plane.

Dr Sheehan's commitment to specific aspects of her subject, such as labour history, the representation of class and the role and portrayal of women will be evident to any reader of this book. This commitment makes her views on classic series such as, on one level, *Strumpet City* and, on another, *The Riordans* and its successor *Glenroe*, valuable insights into historical drama as well as that which attempts to portray a changing Irish society, both urban and rural. The uniqueness of her work in this field for many years has earned her a place in the narrative of Ireland's own unfolding drama.

Richard Pine
Series Editor

Preface

Irish Television Drama: A Society and Its Stories appeared in 1987. It was a story about storytelling. It was a narrative about a society in a process of transformation, about how that social drama played itself out in television drama. That story began in 1962 with the advent of indigenous television, when Radio Telefís Éireann came on air. It moved through twenty-five years of tumult, of a struggle to define the nature of our society and the role of television drama in relation to that.

This book is a sequel to that one. It advances the story another fifteen years. It takes us into the time of the tiger. The tiger in the earlier years was just a feisty cub, smaller and poorer than the rest, but quick to maximise its assets in the game of globalisation. Then came the boom and the flow of milk and honey, cocktails and cappuccinos, megabytes of e-mail and the never ending ringing of mobile phones. There was pride and plenty, but there was also crassness and confusion and exclusion. Living it was one thing, not always as simple as it seemed, but conceptualising it and narrating it were more complex still. Television drama struggled to come to terms with the times, often with considerable confusion, but occasionally with moments of piercing clarity.

In these years much was happening in the world, raising many questions about the relationships of waves of world historical events, the daily flux of experience and the flow of television drama. There have been significant changes, for example, in the climate surrounding broadcasting and in its structures of storytelling: a shift from centralised in-house production to decentralised out-sourced production and co-production; an intensified challenge to public service broadcasting from more commercial forces; the impact of new technological developments such as the internet and digitisation.

In *Irish Television Drama* there were chapters on the nature of narrative and its role in human experience, on television as a medium of drama, on criteria for judging television drama, on contrasting approaches to media studies. I described and defended my theoretical approach as well as my concrete research methods. Subsequent chapters went through each decade, first setting out the temper of the times, then sketching the climate of broadcasting, and finally looking to television drama as the stories this society was telling at this time and place in its development. I have taken as read, rather than reiterating, my theoretical arguments and my explanation of my research methods. I have basically taken the same approach to the last fifteen years as I did to the previous twenty-five.

However, there have been some changes in my methods of research in the intervening years. There was good news and bad news. The good news was computerisation. In those years I got into computers in a way that I never imagined when I was writing my earlier books by hand. First it was word processing for writing my books and articles. A few years later I was creating websites and multimedia productions. The internet has become basic to my connection to the wider world. For this project I found at least some information that I needed on the web. E-mail too was a valuable means of making arrangements and checking facts. The bad news was RTÉ restructuring: the chopping and changing in organisational structures and a scrappy pattern of drama production during this period. The absence of a drama department from 1990 created a sense of discontinuity and made it very difficult in research terms to check facts, trace files, locate continuity of institutional memory and responsibility. Somehow I made my way and found out what I needed to know. I had to learn to find my way around RTÉ again and that was interesting on many levels, from noting new buildings and tracking careers to discovering the story behind the scenes of what I had been watching and catching up on years of showbiz gossip.

There were still the old methods of research, of course. I had watched almost all of this drama on its original transmission and read (and sometimes wrote) the reviews. I had kept up with research in television studies. I gave papers analysing television drama at such events as the International Television Studies Conference in London in 1988 and at the Imagining Ireland Conference at the Irish Film Centre in 1993. I participated in many other such events over the years and benefitted from such interaction as arose. I taught a course on social history and television drama at Dublin City University. When it came to getting down to business on the new book, I made lists, organised interviews, read scripts, reviewed tapes and started writing. While I was writing, there was more drama in production than in many years. I looked in on *Fair City* and *No Tears* when time and circumstance allowed. Conveniently *No Tears* was shooting at DCU.

The publication of the first book has fed back into the loop for the new book. The book was widely reviewed in newspapers and on the airwaves as well as in academic journals. I also got much response to it in conversations and letters. It has had a long shelf-life, being cited in subsequent books, used as a reference source for programme makers and critics and as a text for media courses. It has been a text for one of my own courses at DCU. Each year there was a new set of students before me, which has kept me alert and involved in a process of communicating across generations about television, about our society, about the meaning of life, about the passing of time.

With every onrushing year, events and trends that were matters of contemporary memory have come to be perceived as more distant history.

Students read with near disbelief the story of *The Spike* and find it hard to imagine the RTÉ or Ireland of those times. All the more important then that there should be a written record. I had another reason to remember *The Spike* recently when I was on sabbatical at the University of Cape Town and witnessed something very similar happening in South Africa. *Yizo Yizo* was a television drama set in a township school. A controversy broke out over a sex scene and there were cries from individual viewers and official bodies for it to be taken off the air. Much more than the sex scene was involved, as with *The Spike*. It scrutinised the education system and the society in many aspects. The difference was that times have changed. Also, the South African Broadcasting Corporation and Kader Asmal, the Minister for Education, as well as students and many viewers defended it. Perhaps RTÉ will go again into our schools and even into our universities as well as other such vital institutions of our society and do something courageous and creative with the drama pulsing there.

There is a shift of voice in this book. In the previous book, I used the first person only in the introduction and footnotes. When I was writing about Irish television in the 1960s, it was easier to write entirely in the third person, as I was not living, viewing, working in Ireland during that time. I continued as I started, even though I was living and viewing here during the 1970s and 1980s. When it came to writing about the post-1987 period, it became unnatural. *Irish Television Drama* itself has been part of the public discourse about television drama, and as its author, I was often involved in reviewing new television drama, as well as participating in various programmes and panels on the state of television drama.

This is a difficult country for a critic. It is inevitable that we review and are reviewed by people we know. Too often it degenerates into mutual back-scratching or backstabbing. I have tried to set out my critical criteria and to adhere to them rigorously. I found it interesting after the publication of the previous book that some took this in the spirit in which it was intended, while others, whose work wasn't even so severely criticised, were angry with me for not dealing with their work as they would have wished. Others weighed my arguments and allowed me to believe they were having some impact. My methods of research involved mixing with people whose work I was analysing. I tried to make it clear all along that I was not writing an anecdotal account, a name-dropping list of actors and directors celebrating their performances, nor a glossy coffee table book taking a nostalgic trip through the archives as a PR exercise for RTÉ. It was and is to RTÉ's credit that it commissioned the book with the clear idea that it would be an independent and academic critique. Bob Collins, later director-general of RTÉ, has been particularly affirmative about RTÉ's responsibility to engage with constructive criticism of its work. So I too must be about my own work. This does not mean automatically accepting anyone else's evaluation of it, but it does mean engaging with it on whatever level it deserves. I place it now among a new set of readers and hope for the best.

ACKNOWLEDGEMENTS

I thank those who answered my many questions with grace, reflection, honesty and humour. For chats so full of fun as some of these encounters were, 'interview' seems too stiff a term. Nevertheless, I conducted interviews with Gerard Stembridge, John Lynch, Bob Collins, Farrel Corcoran, Cathal Goan, Mary Callery, Con Bushe, Kevin McHugh, Niall Mathews, David Blake-Knox, Eilis ní Dhuibhne. Not that it was all fun. I was working on this book interviewing Bob Collins on 9–11 when the twin towers were struck. I suspended, for 24 hours, work on *this* drama to deal with *that* drama. Nevertheless I went on 9–12 from the Radio Centre, where I gave one of the most difficult interviews I have ever done, to the RTÉ library to get back on track, even if every conversation for many weeks still moved fitfully from Ireland to the US to Afghanistan. The new academic year brought the usual rhythms of lectures, seminars, meetings, while struggling for research time, punctuated by anti-war teach-ins as well. The research went on into the new season's drama. Of much assistance in making things happen and gathering material at RTÉ were: Peter Feeney, Richard Pine, Clare Duignan, Barbara Durack, Brian Lynch, Malachy Moran, David O'Sullivan, Claire Reynolds.

Aside from RTÉ, the other important institution for me in this sphere has been DCU, as its school of communications has pioneered the discipline of media studies in Ireland and provided me with intellectual stimulation and productive employment. My colleague Eddie Holt, quoted in the text as a television critic, was also someone with whom I had much discussion and many laughs about the world, the university and television. I thank all of my colleagues and students who entered into analysis and arguments about these matters with me. I thank Patrick Kinsella, Séan Phelan and Glenn Gannon for specific assistance. Most of all, I am grateful to Sam Nolan for so many things: videotaping, proofreading, transporting, encouraging, enduring.

Helena Sheehan
Dublin, July 2002

CHAPTER 1

Introduction

THE TIMES FROM 1987 TO 2002

The world turned upside down as the last decade of the twentieth century approached. Whole countries which looked in the late 1980s as if they had a future suddenly ceased to exist in the early 1990s, and a multiplicity of new ones took up their spaces on the map. The cold war was over and a new world order was declared. The first world reigned supreme. The second world disappeared. The third world was all but discarded. Plane loads of westerners headed for the wild east to stake their claims in a new gold rush. Experts came to advise the natives on how to create capitalism and how to build democracy, as if the two were compatible. Prisoners became presidents and presidents became prisoners.

Ireland elected a president who was not only female but feminist. Looking at the world from Ireland, the news and current affairs programmes were full of this drama, even if the fictional characters of its drama took little notice. They continued to grow vegetables and have affairs and buy titles and lived much of the time in a curiously undramatic world, but eventually they too took notice of new times.

The iconic figures of the new right gave way to more subdued successors and then to smooth designer-labelled new social democrats. The hard greed-is-good 80s were said to be giving way to the much nicer 90s. Not that you could tell if you were reading the *Sunday Independent*, where greed was still seen as good and so very glamorous. At least the journalists themselves thought so, propagating a new narcissism, as alien to the faith of their fathers as it was to the brief sojourn of some of them with ideas of socialism and social democracy. *The Keane Edge*[1] was Ireland's *Dallas*. Even they eventually toned it down, catching the new tide after its crest. There were tribunals revealing how those who told the rest of us to tighten our belts lived themselves. We found out the price of the *haute cuisine* and vintage wines they ate and drank, not to mention the mansions, the islands, the stables, the yachts, the helicopters, the

---

1 A social column written by Terry Keane in the *Sunday Independent* during those years.

holidays, even the shirts, they bought. We caught glimpses of the shadowy world in which enormous amounts of money passed hands, even if they found it hard to remember such trivia.

It was an uneven development. In the east greed-is-good only got its time to triumph in the 90s. At first it seemed that obstacles had been cleared and a new creativity was possible. There was talk of a real third way. Then *glasnost* and *perestroika* gave way to mafiacracy. That was not even the worst of it, as a terrible spiral of disintegration fractured harmonious societies into murderous mini-ethnicities. In the other direction, the land of apartheid became the rainbow nation. The wretched of the earth queued for hours in the sun to vote and sang and toyi-toyi-ed and told their stories and forgave those who perse-cuted them, but they still lived in shacks and fainted from hunger and lived in fear. Those who persecuted them did not forgive them and lived behind elec-trified security gates and ate and drank the best of everything and complained about crime and corruption. Things had changed though and some who had lived in shacks went to live in leafy suburbs and drive flash cars and started to think that greed wasn't so bad after all. Besides, there were rules and they were not made by nation states. There was no alternative, almost everyone believed, to the rules of the global economy. Public assets, at least those with the poten-tial for profitability, had to be privatised. It might not be equitable, it might not be efficient, but it just must be. Public health, housing, transport, education were not priorities. Some institutions had intranets and pentium-4s, while others did not have electricity or running water. Virulent viruses, both those that wreaked havoc on computer systems and those that devastated human populations, spread uncontrollably. The AIDS statistics for Africa became alarming.

Globalisation swept all before it. Globalisation and fragmentation para-doxically went together. All the old ties that bound loosened and gave way. Local communities, political movements, nation states, public service broad-casting were a shadow of what they were, but, never mind, you could buy a Big Mac anywhere. The communications revolution rolled on. Anyone who couldn't get e-mail or surf the web or send text messages on their mobile phone just wasn't with it. The world really was connected in a whole new way through the internet.

The Asian tigers roared in youthful exuberance, strutted their stuff on the world stage and then collapsed into a shambling quotidian hunt. Then a Celtic cub came into the clearing and was much more charming and better behaved. Rising tides lifted many boats. There was a building boom. Construction workers, long queuing for the dole, had more work than they could handle and it was hard to walk ten steps without walking by a building site. Recruitment fairs were held in far flung places as a land of emigration became a place of immigration. People of many colours queued for buses on O'Connell Street. Seminars were organised on multiculturalism, refugees and racism. New forms of Irish culture stepped up and strode across the world stage, whether in song (U2, the Corrs, Sinead O'Connor) or in film (*The Commitments, The Crying Game, In the Name of the Father, Dancing at Lughnasa*). Temple Bar in Dublin city centre became the new left bank. New buildings and cultural institutions shot up and tourists came from far and wide. It was the place to be for film, music, multimedia, stand-up comedy and foreign stag parties.

There were changes of government in Ireland and Britain and a peace process and new institutions in Northern Ireland. There was a new level of scrutiny of older institutions of church and state. Media exposés and tribunals shed a light on the dark secrets of the days gone by. The stories of priests and bishops and their sons and lovers shocked the nation at first, but then came a torrent of tales about where consecrated hands had been and about children who carried on confused and abused. The faith of our fathers was no longer ours, no matter how well the CD sold. *Nothing Sacred, Priest, Father Ted*, dramas of priests fallen from pedestals, hounded off screens by Catholics in America, were lauded in Ireland. Truly nothing was sacred any more.

A sharp struggle of opposites had played itself out in the preceding decades, but what had come of this vigorous dialectic was not a vibrant new synthesis but an insipid eclecticism. Right and left were declared irrelevant and everyone crowded into the centre with nothing very interesting to say or do there. The big ideas, insofar as there were any, were the debris of previous decades. Postmodernism made the zanier recombinations seem chic some-times, but there was really a kind of hopelessness in the flux, a desperation to fill the empty space with anything at all. Generation x and y and z felt that all the great causes had already been fought, that all the good lines had already been written, that all the good songs had already been sung. Universities were reined in to serve the needs of the market. Philosophy departments closed down, but *Sophie's World* topped the best seller list in country after country.

Without communists to threaten it, the 'free world' was suddenly full of aliens to expose and vampires to slay and rogue nations to deter and terrorists to decimate. The last alas were real. The scenario lived already in the popular imagination of the time with multiplying fictional images of architectural icons of political, financial and military power exploding spectacularly. The new rulers of the world sketched a manichean world of good-versus-evil and all were told they must take sides. If you did not stand with the USA, which had the right to call the shots for the whole world, you were with the terrorists. The nation state was not what it was, but, for the one surviving superpower, it could be what it wanted and no one seemed to have the power to say otherwise.

The millennium, along with the Y2K scare, came and went, and the year 2000 was very like 1999. 2001 was different altogether. A normal day – 11 September – began and catastrophe struck and the world prepared for a weird war. Jihad versus McWorld[2] was drawing blood and creating world historical havoc. Television drama was suspended for a night, then came back with what was in the can, eerily showing on the skyline buildings that were gone. *The West Wing* and *Third Watch* put new episodes into production to reflect the new reality. The playgrounds of privilege became precarious. The masters of the universe discovered their vulnerability, but did not extend their gaze much beyond vengeance and the singularity of their own suffering and still did not understand how the rest of the world lived and suffered. Capitalism appealed to non-capitalist values. God was claimed to be on both sides, as in most wars. Public servants briefly became public heroes. Even earlier in 2001 there was talk of slowdown, even recession, as the factory closures began again. Was the time of the tiger over?

RTÉ FROM 1987 TO 2002

There were many changes in the climate of broadcasting during these years. Globally there was increased concentration of media ownership and further weakening of public service broadcasting. Legislation enacted in 1988 and 1990 legalised private television broadcasting and diverted revenue from the public to the private sector. RTÉ struggled to navigate a continued commitment to public service broadcasting while becoming more commercial in response to increased competition from many directions. Production costs continued to rise, while the licence fee didn't and advertising revenue was capped.[3] The justification was 'to level the playing pitch'. A decade later, tribunals began to throw light on shady relationships between the government of the time and the commercial interests involved. The minister responsible, Ray Burke of Fianna Fáil, was discredited. Even when he was in office, *Scrap Saturday*[4] characterised him as 'a confidence trickster called Rambo, due to his gung-ho attitude and unpleasant demeanour', commenting on his broadcasting legislation: 'While he offered the pitch for sale, he was unaware what the game was, who wanted to play, how to score or anything else. He just wanted to see RTÉ take a hiding.'

Amending legislation by a new government in 1993 removed the cap, but compelled RTÉ to spend an escalating proportion of its annual budget on independent production. This was a global trend. It was also a requirement for

---

2 Benjamin Barber, *Jihad vs. McWorld: How Globalism and Tribalism are Reshaping the World* (New York: Ballantine, 1996).   3 In 1990 Minister for Communications Ray Burke introduced a 'cap' or maximum amount which RTÉ was allowed to earn from advertising revenue.   4 A satirical radio programme broadcast on RTÉ Radio 1, 1990–2 (see below, pp. 21–2).

the BBC. The EU enforced deregulation within the EU, but subsidised audio-visual projects to reinforce European culture against the ongoing tide of Hollywoodisation. The *Television without Frontiers* directive in 1989 created a single internal market.

Some of those who came to positions of power in broadcasting in Ireland in the 1990s were seriously committed to public service broadcasting and to rearticulating it in light of the new challenges to it, which they well understood. Michael D. Higgins, Labour TD and prominent public intellectual, became Minister for Arts, Culture and the Gaeltacht in the government formed in 1993. Farrel Corcoran, Professor of Communications at Dublin City University (DCU), was appointed chair of the RTÉ Authority in 1995. Bob Collins was appointed Director-General of RTÉ in 1997. In 1995 the government published a green paper entitled *Active or Passive? Broadcasting in the Future Tense.*[5]

Both the green paper and RTÉ's response to it engaged in discourse about the future of broadcasting at a high intellectual level with a vigorous polemic about what was at stake for the very character of the social order. There were sarcastic remarks made around RTÉ and elsewhere about obscure quotations from Habermas, but the green paper was a lucid defence of the public sphere against the market liberalism prevailing in the USA and the EU. It stressed the necessity to defend public space and to address the audience primarily as citizens rather than as consumers. It championed multicultural diversity and the inclusion of all voices in a national dialogue. While RTÉ appreciated and accepted the commitment to public service broadcasting, it opposed its proposal to set up a super-authority that would merge the RTÉ Authority, the IRTC (Independent Radio and Television Commission set up in 1988) and the Broadcasting Complaints Commission.[6] In 1997 the government published a white paper entitled *Clear Focus: Proposals for Broadcasting Legislation*[7] giving clear legal definition to public service broadcasting and putting forward an Irish Broadcasting Commission.

However, after the election of 1997, there was a Fianna Fáil-Progressive Democrat government again and Síle de Valera was a very different type of minister to Michael D. Higgins. Nevertheless, during his time as minister, much happened. The much criticised Section 31[8] was finally revoked in 1994. The Irish Film Board was reinstated in 1993. Telefís na Gaeilge (TnaG, subsequently renamed TG4), based in Connemara, came on air in 1996, heavily subsidised by government and nurtured by RTÉ. The IPU (Independent Productions Unit) was set up in RTÉ in 1993 to develop, commission and fund programmes from independent production companies. Meanwhile, Tara TV and Celtic Vision brought Irish programmes to cable subscribers in Britain and America.

5 Dublin: Government Stationery Office, 1995. **6** RTÉ, *Response to the Government's Green Paper on Broadcasting* (Dublin: RTÉ, 1995). **7** Dublin: Government Stationery Office, 1997. **8** Section 31 of the Broadcasting Act (1960) empowered the government to issue directives to the RTÉ Authority prohibiting the broadcasting of specific material, most usually by members of organisations deemed to be 'subversive'.

The much expected and long delayed arrival of Irish commercial television came in 1998. TV3 made little contribution to national culture and none in the area of drama. The bulk of its programmes were imported, some of them already available on other channels. RTÉ need not have worried. However, after Granada Television purchased a large minority shareholding in TV3,[9] it did outbid RTÉ for *Coronation Street*, with the result that *EastEnders* – up to then transmitted by TV3 – was acquired by RTÉ. TV3's indigenous programming, such as it was, was derivative, clumsy and shallow, although *Agenda* was sometimes astute. Much of the commercial sector in broadcasting, despite its stated aims of being an indigenous alternative, has passed quickly into foreign ownership.[10]

Basically it was a time of considerable change, which created in RTÉ an atmosphere of uncertainty, much of it deriving from insecurity about the funding of broadcasting.[11] In 2001 RTÉ was finally granted an increase in licence fee, but it was substantially less than proposed. In these years there was a decisive shift from in-house to independent production and co-production. The line between co-production and commissioned production became porous, as many co-productions between RTÉ and the BBC were actually made by independent production companies. The uncertainty also derived from an unresolved tension between public service and commercial pressures. Analysing the state of RTÉ in 1995, Fintan O'Toole observed that it sometimes seemed to be the worst of both worlds, combining a culture of caution and self-censorship with a more commercial mentality in its preoccupation with advertising revenue, competition and ratings:

> it seemed to have all the susceptibility to political caution of a state organisation with none of the protection from market pressures and all the drive towards vulgar consumerism of a commercial station with none of the populist energy. A purely commercial station would never have dropped *Scrap Saturday*, which got huge audience and ... advertising revenue. A purely public service station would never have turned RTÉ Radio 2 ... into 2FM, a pop station virtually indistinguishable from its commercial rivals ... While talking about the need for innovative programmes appealing to a younger audience, RTÉ dropped the most successful of such programmes *Nighthawks*.[12]

The climate of uncertainty was particularly manifest in drama production.

9 45% of TV3 was owned by CanWest Global Communications Corporation. In 2000 most of the remaining Irish-owned shares were purchased by Granada Television, which now has a 45% stake in the company. **10** For example, Scottish Media Holdings and UTV have moved to purchase control of several local radio stations. **11** Interviews with Farrel Corcoran and Bob Collins, both on 11 September 2001. **12** Fintan O'Toole, *Irish Times* 4 November 1995.

CHAPTER 2

RTÉ drama

After the vigorous debate about RTÉ drama during the 1980s,[1] there was a sense that something decisive would be done. Instead, what followed was perhaps the most indecisive period in its history. There was constant chopping and changing. There was loss of confidence that RTÉ could do drama. It lurched from one experiment to another, then scrapped each one and acted as if it were starting from zero with the next. There was almost a sense of desperation about it, manifested in such decisions as bringing in foreign expertise to produce indigenous drama, most strikingly in the development of the new urban serial. Instead of building on existing expertise, developing new talent, producing critical mass and doing so having a clear sense of what role RTÉ drama should be playing in relation to 1990s Irish society, there was a grasping at straws, followed by a barrage of criticism, followed by drama drying up for a time and then trying again.

During this period RTÉ produced less drama than ever and what it did produce was tamer than ever. Soap opera was the only constant through this period. The 1991 annual report acknowledged that there was a lacuna in the area of drama. There were several television discussions on the state of television drama in Ireland, particularly *Down the Tube* in 1989 and *Feedback* in 1994. I was on both and argued that RTÉ was floundering, that it needed focus and fire. Robert Carrickford of Equity said that Ireland was in the third world as far as drama output was concerned. Eugene McCabe urged RTÉ to do drama of contemporary life and not do *The Rose of Tralee*. Michael Colgan said of RTÉ in 1989: 'They cannot go on like this.'

DRAMA DEPARTMENT AND SINGLE PLAYS

In 1988 there was still a drama department. Noel O'Briain was head of drama. There was a short-lived sense of a new start for drama. Plans for the future

1 See Sheehan, *Irish Television Drama*, Chapter 6.

involved expansion of *Glenroe*, an urban serial and a return of the single play. The midweek play slot for original television plays was launched in 1988 with four plays. The scripts were ones for which RTÉ had previously acquired rights, but for one reason or other had never gone into production.

Tom Murphy's *Brigit* was set in 1930s rural Ireland and shed a light on the harshness of peasant economy and emotion. It concerned a woodcutter named Séamus who was in dispute with the church over unpaid work and was keeping his grandchildren away from mass in protest. When commissioned to produce a statue of Brigit to replace a statue of the saint that had been broken by a young nun in the convent, he carved from bog oak a strong and primitive image. When the mother superior demanded that he paint it, he refused, again leaving him without desperately needed payment. His wife, named Brigit, with whom his relationship had grown so cold that he had not called her by name for many years, was first angry about the money, but then came to see value in this creation and a new bond developed between them. For Fintan O'Toole:

> In *Brigit*, official religion is a dead thing and the story is Séamus' attempt at a personal replacement based on the immediate life around him … The immediate struggle with the past, which Murphy drama- tised in the changing world of the sixties, is over, but there remains a past with which there is not so immediate a connection, the past of all the voiceless generations of the poor who have suffered in silence … Séamus in *Brigit*, both in his character and in his statue, is an image of all that suffering and endurance.[2]

It was a charming and meaningful folk tale. While it was not a tract for the times in an obvious way, it did provide a stark reflection on aspects of the past with which the present needed to bear a connection.

The others were more contemporary, but not exactly cutting edge. Bernard Farrell's *Lotty Coyle Loves Buddy Holly* showed an older woman who didn't believe that her later years should be spent waiting for the hearse. She found joy in pop music and even autumn romance against the opposition of her upwardly mobile family. It was light and unpretentious, but marred by a tendency to see manual labourers as somehow inherently funny and by some clumsy lines and cheap laughs.

Lee Gallaher's *Errors and Omissions*, described as 'a mood piece which makes its revelations in an uncompromising way' and 'in the tradition of European cinema', looked at the relationship of two middle-aged women and

2 Fintan O'Toole, *The Politics of Magic* (Dublin: Raven Arts Press, 1987) pp. 182–3.

the impact of the arrival of a niece who had been travelling around Europe with her American boyfriend. However, it failed to make its revelations to me. There seemed to be an assumption that silences somehow evoked profundity. There was some texture to it with the *New Statesman*, Noel Browne's autobiography, Mozart's piano concertos and bits of French in it, but somehow it felt pointless, as they seemed parasitic self-indulgent people over-indulged by the script.

Brian Mitchell's *The Black Knight*, a thriller set in Belfast, put RTÉ in an arena usually left to the BBC and ITV. It was an unsolicited script centred on the attempt of a son of a wealthy businessman, on his return from travelling around the continent, to create a cultural space that would take people's minds off the troubles and make a new life for himself. Bringing the Berlin tradition of political cabaret to Belfast didn't quite work though, either in the story or in the production.

There was a sense that the drama department was trying to meet the criticism that had been laid at its door by going back to the past instead of looking to the future. It was felt that drama had to be organised in a new way and that the drama department had become too conservative and too exclusive in its approach to television drama.

YOUTH AND EXPERIMENTAL DRAMA

From 1990 on the drama department was closed (some said it 'evaporated') and drama was grouped with entertainment and young people's programming. The area of young people's programming was a continuing source of some of the more innovative drama, for example, with *Finbarr's Class* running for two series in 1995 and 1996, a '*Fame* meets *The Spike*' chalk opera.[3] Also there were slots such as *Scene*, *First View* and *Debut* for newcomers to programme-making.

Most innovative and interesting were several series of dramas, developed in workshop with young actors, written and directed by Gerard Stembridge. The first series was called *Nothing to It*. It revolved around flatmates living in a Dublin bedsit ready to start being what they wanted to be when they grew up, if only they could figure out what they wanted to be. Each week they would imagine themselves into a career and their imagined lives in that career would be played out experimentally. It was full of irony and fun, but it also touched tellingly on Irish society at various points in exploring, even in young people's caricatures, the lives of gardaí, politicians, civil servants, journalists, bankers, caterers and computer experts. Woven through the series was the sort of

3 For discussion of *The Spike*, see H. Sheehan, op. cit., pp. 162–77.

advice given to teenagers for decades, but sounding somewhat ridiculous by the late 1980s, by agony aunt Agnes Day (the first of many televisual incarnations of Pauline McLynn).

The next series in 1988 was called *Commonplaces*. It was organised around a fictional government scheme for community drama. In each episode, in a play-within-a-play scenario, each of the five fictional characters, five unemployed young people, created their own fictional characters and the group would work out and enact a story around them. Among these characters were: a Slade fan searching for the one record needed to have a complete collection; a housewife addicted to valium and *Neighbours*, who was caught up in Mills & Boon and *Dynasty* fantasies for transforming her life; a pirate radio disc jockey coming to terms with the current affairs requirements in the new legalised broadcasting environment. There was also, lo and behold, a communist, a young man who sold the *Irish Socialist* on O'Connell Bridge (with Joan Baez singing *We Shall Overcome* on the soundtrack) and attended party meetings in Dublin, who withdrew for a time to the Botanic Gardens, while pursued by comrades and special branch detectives asking him to explain himself. These were improvisational without being tacky. They were humourous without being frivolous. They were marked by good performances, intelligent imagination and an authentic feel for urban life in the late eighties.

The Truth about Claire

More ambitious and intricate was *The Truth about Claire*, again developed in workshop and written, produced and directed by Gerard Stembridge. It was in five parts and transmitted over two nights in 1991. The surface story was that a young woman named Claire from a small town in Cork, who had married at 18, had two children and was expecting her third at 26, came to Dublin to stay with a school friend Denise, who was an executive in an ad agency. She met various people in Denise's circle, flew to London, had an abortion, then came home and killed herself. The first four parts consisted in interviews with four characters who knew her during the two weeks before she died when she was in Dublin.

A documentary was being made about why Claire Twomey died. All through the production was the presence of the documentary film-maker asking the questions during the interviews and editing them afterwards. Each of the four characters told the story from their own point of view and key scenes were enacted and re-enacted from the perspective of the character telling it. There were not only subtle differences of emphasis, but contradictory versions of events. In between, there were degrees of misapprehension and cluelessness. It started with the character least implicated in events, David, a separated man with children, a lodger in Denise's suburban house. He was unaware of much of what was happening and, after it happened, wondered: 'Do you have to make it mean something?' The second was Paul, a teacher, who campaigned in 1983 for the constitutional amendment to guarantee the right to life of the unborn. He believed that abortion was murder and tried to dissuade Claire from having an abortion. He contended that she was a victim of 'the way society is going now'. The third was Colman, a freelance journalist on the make, who played one against another and tried to manipulate Claire into letting him make a documentary on her experience. He blamed everyone else. The fourth was Denise, her friend, who had been drifting through her yuppie life and found meaning in these events in that they shook everything up and made her see how pathetic it all was. In the argument that took place at the dinner table on the issue of abortion, Denise had taken on Paul, saying: 'What do you know about it on any level? How dare you sit there like some pussy faced curate? Mother Ireland, you are rearing them yet.' She did advise Claire to have an abortion, but argued that her death had nothing to do with abortion.

The fifth part was the documentary called *The Truth about Claire: An Irish Tragedy*. It was a vivid lesson in the power and possibilities of editing. The overt edit was a documentary slanted to the anti-abortion, anti-liberal, anti-urban point of view. It showed Paul, for example, whom we had seen all untogether in himself, insensitive to the needs and motives of others and tetchy and insulting to pupils, looking as if he were a lucid person, sympathetic friend and committed teacher. It contrasted a wholesome family life and rural society with the hustle of individuals torn apart in the city. It did not answer the question of why Claire died, but it presented the evidence available in a certain way. As the credits came up, the soundtrack carried some of the out-takes in Claire's own voice, which cast the story in a very different light, although still not compelling a definitive answer.

This, I believed at the time and still do looking back on it now, was what RTÉ could and should have been doing in its drama. It was not an argument for what is called (and caricatured as) issue-based drama. The point to me was not that it was about abortion. It was that it was about our society in a thought-provoking and emotionally engaging way. It was dramatising different points of view and ways of life and orchestrating them in relation to each other. It was, to be fair, what RTÉ was perhaps trying to do in its other drama productions, but with diminishing effectiveness.

RTÉ AND COMEDY

In various experiments in comedy the basic idea was to look at Irish society and to highlight the various ways of life and attitudes to the world that existed in awkward and ironic juxtaposition with each other. Much of the discontent about RTÉ had to do with the dearth of comedy and of urban drama. Both *Leave It to Mrs O'Brien* and *Inside* were attempts to meet both needs simultaneously. Both failed to do either. Still RTÉ kept trying.

Molloy

Molloy was a six-part comedy serial in 1989, which revolved around the character of Mick Molloy, a 47-year-old working-class man who had forgotten how to work. Unemployment had become normal and even comfortable. He had been an honest worker put on the scrap heap by a firm that went bankrupt in Ireland, only to resurface in India, where it would not have to deal with trade unions and pay a living wage. He did not let bitterness over this get the better of him. He had settled into a way of life built around the consolations of reading books, watching television documentaries, philosophising about the capitalist system and enjoying the pints and *craic* of Dublin pub culture.

The relative equilibrium of this life was then disrupted when he was offered work. His attempt at a solution to his dilemma was to persuade his mate, who had not been so long out of work and so cosily accommodated to unemployment, to impersonate him. It all came to grief and all had their say: his long-suffering wife, his hostile mother-in-law, his five children trying to make their own way in the world, his neighbours who had been implicated.

It was written by Paul O'Loughlin, who left school at 14, worked at various jobs, but had also been unemployed. After accumulating a pile of rejection slips, this was his first script to be accepted. This in itself was interesting in that it occurred in a broadcasting climate in which the odds were mounting against writers without previous experience and without connections. It was the sort of effort many wanted to succeed. When I first reviewed it after the second episode, I stressed everything in its favour I could find.[4] My worst fears about it had been relieved. It did not reduce urban culture to lumpen subculture, as did *Bread* on BBC or *Inside* on RTÉ. Unemployment was seen as basically sad and not inherently funny. Molloy had been unemployed so long as to be nearly unemployable, but he was not lumpen. The other characters, some of whom not only lived in the city, but actually worked, encompassed a wide range and were played against each other in terms of differences in class, gender, generation and ideological attitudes.

The problem was that these tended to be expressed in a throwaway way. It was not sharp enough to be challenging. Another problem was that it seemed to treat the very expression of political or philosophical views as somehow deviant or escapist and certainly always male. In the relationship between Mick and Mary Molloy, she was the rock, dealing with reality. Reality was defined as bread

---

4 Helena Sheehan, 'Comedy' in the *New Nation* 4 (1989). I also reviewed *Molloy* on *The Arts Show* on RTÉ Radio 1 and *Down the Tube* on RTÉ Television.

and rashers and not economic systems. It did not cast a satirical eye on the traditional sexual division of labour, but privileged the pre-feminist female position.

There were some funny lines:

Mary Molloy (*his wife*): Sure, he's his own worst enemy.
Maureen Ryan (*his mother-in-law*): Not so long as I'm alive.

However, on the whole, it was not funny enough to be good comedy and it
didn't have a compelling enough narrative to be good drama. The final
episode, which producer-director Tom McArdle promised would be the fun-
niest, involved the neighbours donning balaclavas and kidnapping Molloy and
demanding a ransom and the wife saying that she didn't want him back and
going off on holiday with the daughter. Even looking at it again, asking if I had
been too harsh when I reviewed it at the end, it seemed lame. Those involved
in this production did want to hold a mirror up to our society, especially to the
problems of working class life, and to say something serious and something
funny about it, but perhaps should have taken longer in development with it.

Extra Extra Read All About It
The next effort at a sitcom was in 1993. It was called *Extra Extra Read All About
It*. It was a series of six episodes set in the newsroom of a Sunday newspaper
called *The Bugle*. The characters included the editor, a social columnist, an arts
editor cum agony aunt (male), reporters and an accountant. It was a good idea.
After all, so much of human life comes through a newsroom. There are the journalists who work there plus all those whose stories are processed there. There is
the bonding and the conflict of the workplace plus scope for ironic querying of
the news agenda, the possibilities of editing and so much more. It can honestly be
said that RTÉ got it wrong in this case. There were gags about going tabloid and
having 'page three girls', about trade unions, about marketing, about television
listings, about office parties. The problem was that they just weren't that funny.

The whole enterprise was superficial, unengaging, embarrassing. In a class
of future journalists (doing the BA in Journalism at DCU) in a lecture on satirical images of journalists, I showed scenes from *Extra Extra* alongside scenes
from *Murphy Brown, Drop the Dead Donkey* and *The Newsroom* (from CBC in
Canada and shown on RTÉ's Network 2). Students poured scorn on RTÉ and
I struggled to defend it against one (or more) bad productions. There was
much work put into its development in workshops, but 'creative differences'
developed and some who had been working on it left in anger and it went into
production amidst all these tensions. It was panned in the press.[5]

---

5 Interviews with John Lynch, 18 August 2001, and David Blake-Knox, 22 and 23 August 2001.

Upwardly Mobile

The next sitcom ran for four series from 1995 to 1998. It was called *Upwardly Mobile*. It opened with painted scenes of Dublin and a catchy tune:

> So it's goodbye to old Arthur J
> And *bonjour* to fine chablis
> I am leaving my heart at the Ha'penny Bridge
> Now it's Belvedere for me.

The scenario was one where two households of different class origins existed next door to each other as a result of upward mobility on the part of a working-class family who won the Lotto. They were played against each other in comedic contrast. It had been done a number of times and RTÉ even did it itself in 1975 in *Up in the World*, but they possibly forgot (or didn't read my book). This was a period of discontinuity of institutional memory when new teams were constantly seeing themselves as starting again from scratch. This particular attempt had been devised in an RTÉ sitcom writing seminar and passed through various hands before coming to air.

The basic story was that Dublin working-class inner-city northsiders won £2 million on the Lotto and moved to south county suburbia. When Eddie and Molly Keogh left De Valera Mansions and arrived in Belvedere Downs, their lives came into juxtaposition with those of Anthony and Pamela Moriarty. The characters were crude stereotypes and the gags were often based on stage-Dublin accents and the most superficial markers of class and gender differentiation. They did not say anything sharp or interesting about class or gender. Some of the working class characters bordered on the moronic. Sex was a matter of constant vulgar innuendo:

> — I've always been very good with balls, Eddie.
> — Mollo, a few nibbles …
> — It's time you stopped playing with yourself.

It was made with a live audience and did not use canned laughter on the soundtrack. There were allegations by a critic that alchohol consumption in the green room prior to recording explained the laughs for unfunny gags. This was denied by its executive producer who contended that arrangements for audience hospitality were the same as for *The Late Late Show* or *Kenny Live*. David Blake-Knox went on to say that the *Evening Herald* critic Peter Howick might not be a fan of the series, but 750,000 Irish people who watched it had a different view. He then remarked on the subhead given to the review 'Downwardly unfunny at *Upwardly Mobile*' and swiped 'So *that's* the sort of gag that gets you guys laughing'.[6] All the same it was sometimes hard to know how it got its laughs. For example, in a pub scene:

> — I love Christmas. (*laughter*)
> — Shopping, that's women's stuff. (*laughter*)

The humour did not bite. Critic Eddie Holt, after reviewing it as unfunny in its first season, came back to it in its third season and took it to task as being 'too timid, too afraid to say anything meaningful about class.'[7]

David Blake-Knox, who had primary responsibility for the development of drama during this period, first as group head of the drama, variety and young people's departments and then as director of television production, as well as being executive producer of *Upwardly Mobile*, admitted that RTÉ did not really crack this genre. He stressed that it was a particularly difficult genre, comparing it to a pyramid and arguing that it was necessary to have the critical mass of many projects in development to have any that got to the top in quality. He pointed to the situation in Britain, where there might be 100 projects in development, 30 or 40 a year going to air, 10 renewed for another year and only 2 or 3 to survive beyond that.[8]

SITCOM, SATIRE AND IRISH SOCIETY

This has been part of the problem in developing comedy at RTÉ. There is considerable humour pervading everyday life in Ireland, but there has rarely been the time and effort and finance to raise this natural resource to the level of art. If we look at any of the television comedy from abroad that we see and admire on our screens and then look at the credits at the end and see the number of writers and others whose talents have been channelled into it and compare it to an RTÉ production, the gap is obvious. Several years at a time were let to pass and then in the case of *Molloy* one inexperienced writer was left to carry it. We have been long accustomed to sharp, sophisticated and sometimes hard-hitting comedy on our television screens and we bring all the expectations this has engendered to our indigenous productions. This puts a heavy burden on RTÉ with an inevitable problem of scale, but until comparable resources are put into it, there will be a constant cycle of disappointment in this area. This alone does not explain it, however. It is not an adequate excuse for the timidity and the blandness, for the failure to satirise the contradictions

---

6 Peter Howick, *Evening Herald*, 8 November 1996; David Blake-Knox, *Evening Herald*, 13 November 1996. **7** Eddie Holt, *Irish Times*, 20 September 1997. **8** Interview with David Blake-Knox, 22 August 2001.

of Irish society, particularly the pretensions of those in power, as it emerged into the era of the so-called Celtic tiger. It was starting to be said that RTÉ and comedy were a contradiction in terms.

RTÉ did have some successes in satirical production. On radio, there was *Scrap Saturday* from 1990 to 1992, which became central to the public discourse. Its creators, Dermot Morgan and Gerard Stembridge, expected that it might have a cult following, but the scale of response was unexpected. It captured the popular imagination and pushed out the parameters of what was permissible in the realm of political and social satire. It went further than any of its predecessors on the airwaves and got away with it, at least for a time. Any hostility to it was reduced to near silence, which was eerie. It may have been that the balance of forces had changed in favour of what the show was doing, but the lack of public debate about it was not healthy. It was part of a sea change in Irish society, coinciding with the election of Mary Robinson as president. The most explicit attack on it was done with the most astonishing ineptitude and ignorance. Madeleine Taylor Quinn TD was like a daft child stumbling into a minefield. Based on garbled accounts from her constituents and without the most elementary understanding of the satirical nature of the programme, she went on to the nation's airwaves to complain about RTÉ carrying an ad for Sky News trivialising the Gulf War. From then on the programme targetted her. 'MTQ' missiles were not considered to be smart weapons.

It wasn't only those who attacked who became targets. What was more remarkable was the way the programme took on even those who praised and promoted them, quite amazing in a society in which there was so much shameless toadying and mutual back-scratching. It was Mike Murphy who gave Dermot Morgan his start as a media comedian in the days of *Live Mike*, and yet the jovial lightweight levelling banality of his role as arts presenter was a running theme. He enthused over Shakespeare: 'he's really *in* right now'. Gay Byrne too gave Dermot Morgan a most sympathetic platform on *The Late Late Show* and *The Gay Byrne Show*, and played a selection of his favourite sketches at the end of the first season, yet they began portraying him as vain, cynical, manipulative, condescending and parasitic on the grief of others. Even the radio audience itself got taken on, with GB being besieged by 'every menopausal old one in the country looking for a washing machine'.

No one could say that they went for easy targets. All the institutions of church and state and civil society were considered fair game, including those with most power over their own lives: 'And now on RTÉ, your only national broadcasting station, we bring you your only national religion ...' RTÉ programme formats were used as vehicles, not only for satirising RTÉ's own programmes and presenters, but for opening out to the whole society as mediated by the media. Other media formats too were appropriated, such as the Hollywood trailer: '*Our Left President* ... the story of a woman who gave up socialism for love'. Newspapers were combed both for form and content, *The Keane Edge* column especially. No person or institution, dead or alive, home or abroad, could be considered safe, especially when Eamon Dunphy was allowed to rant about everything from the weather to the history of philosophy. Even Mother Teresa: 'a tea towel on your head and good works with India's lower castes doesn't make a nun'. The relationship of poetry to power was a recurrent theme: Richard Kearney's poem celebrating the accession of Noel Davern as Minister for Education and Brendan Kennelly's preparation for performance at Kinsealy: 'I thought I would use the metaphor of the Toyota to suggest the powerful movement of the Haughey factor.'

From a different ideological position, there was Fintan O'Toole explaining how Abbey plays should be 'like my newspaper articles, only with dialogue'. Brendan and Caitriona, symbols of an Ireland on the run, came into it with a new SPUC sex video. The Provisional IRA and the GAA were targets, as was Eoghan Harris quoting Marx to Fine Gael as he coached them for the introduction of television cameras in the Dáil. Politicians were a prominent presence, particularly those of the party in power. The CJ–PJ[9] dialogues provided a picture of Charles Haughey that intuitively seemed far truer than that of his public persona and much more interesting as well. In the outpouring of sugary sentimentality that filled the newspaper pages when Haughey finally did fall from his position as Fianna Fáil party leader, when even some of our most respected commentators lost the run of themselves altogether, Morgan did not recant. Later revelations vindicated the *Scrap Saturday* view of Haughey all the more.

The programme was designed to break the barriers. Dermot Morgan said that he decided to go for broke, to pull no punches. He did not consider it to be a bit of harmless fun. He saw himself as 'a political activist on stage' and believed that his strongest work came from his deepest anger. *Scrap Saturday* came out of a long smouldering rage at the state of Irish society, 'the pettiness, the greyness of it all', the stifling influence of the church, the excess of self-esteem radiated by politicians.[10] There were icons that just had to be shattered and he was proud to be their iconoclast. *Scrap Saturday* was conceived in a deep inner necessity and brought catharsis. Not everyone got every joke. Not everybody had to get every joke. I have to admit that some of the sporting references passed me by, as some of the political, philosophical or literary

---

9 Satirising Charles J. Haughey and his spokesman P. J. Mara.   10 Interviews with Dermot Morgan and Gerard Stembridge in 1992; also H. Sheehan, 'The parameters of the pemissible: how *Scrap Saturday* got away with it', *Irish Communications Review*, 1992 and 'End of Scrap leaves void in Irish satire', *Sunday Press*, 5 January 1992.

references may have been lost on others. This was part of the cleverness of the programme: that it could work on a number of different levels and appeal to diverse sections of the audience. It could reach a mass audience without reducing itself to the least common denominator to do so.

What those who made it wanted was to take it to television, but it was dropped all together. RTÉ would only say that it had run its course and would not admit that there was any political heat. I tried at the time to pin down what was really behind this decision.[11] Years later, probing it further, Bob Collins, subsequently director-general, told me that it got caught in a variety of currents, that there was apprehension that it had crossed the boundaries. There was heat, but it was totally ignorable and it should have been ignored, he said.[12]

Nighthawks

Running at the same time on television was *Nighthawks*. This was one of the boldest and most innovative programmes RTÉ has ever made. It pushed hard at the boundaries of what could be done in the way of social and political satire. It was a mixed format live show set in a fictional café, involving satirical sketches, current affairs interviews, cultural reviews, conversations, music and ironic interactions of real personalities with fictional ones. It went out on Network 2 three nights a week from 1988 to 1992. As well as its 350 episodes, it spawned several spin-offs, such as *The Confessions of Bláithín Keaveney* in 1990 and *A Song for Europe* in 1991; both of these were spoofs of the early days of Telefís Éireann. The Bláithín character was a frequent continuity persona on *Nighthawks*, appearing in black and white in dated production style, announcing features such as a documentary on an Irish priest: 'If you've ever wanted to know what's up a young priest's cassock ...'

Media formats, old and new, were turned inside out. There were recurring appearances of Éamon de Valera in MTV spots:

> Sing gloria, sing gloria
> For the one, holy, catholic and apostolic church ...

There was a fad at the time, pioneered by Paula Yates on *The Big Breakfast* on Channel 4 and copied by various Irish journalists in the pages of the *Sunday Independent*, of doing interviews in beds. *Nighthawks* showed the president of Ireland, Mary Robinson, being interviewed by four young men in a bed, explaining, 'I want my house to be for marginalised people' to which one of the

---

11 Interview with John P. Kelly, commissioning editor at RTÉ, 1992.   **12** Interview with Bob Collins, 11 September 2001.

young men replied, 'Sounds like a bar I know'. Another had Mary R explaining that it wasn't really necessary to memorise Paul Durcan poems, because all you had to do was to speak ordinary sentences and say 'backside' a lot and pause in the wrong places. There was a *Jo-Maxi* competition to find a new name for the Workers Party with a trip to Moscow as the prize. There was a *Today-Tonight* feature on 'forgotten leaders of our time' showing how Alan Dukes, once leader of Fine Gael, was now playing backing guitar for Lulu.

There was a documentary on a transvestite farmer, which showed Sean, dressed in frilly dresses and stilettos, driving a tractor, carrying bales of hay, shovelling slurry, with the voice-over talking about GATT agreements, competition from Eastern Europe, computerisation of farm management, and concluding that 'hard work might not be enough'. There were discussions among Irish bishops done as if they were episodes of *The Golden Girls*. It called attention to the incongruity between what bishops said and how they dressed and implied some of them were in it for the clothes. Other regular sketches showed Cork people in space and Saint Martina of Marley Park. There was an initiative to engage in male prostitution to raise funds for the GAA.

It should have gone on and on. However, various people who were working on it wanted to spin off in different directions and thought that it would be easier to do so than it proved to be. David Bake-Knox, producer and then television executive, admitted that it should have continued until there was something comparable to put in its place.[13] *Extra Extra Read All About It* was a failed attempt to spin off from it.

The audience who had been screaming for *Scrap Saturday* or something like it on television finally got *Bull Island* in 1999. It featured political and cultural sketches. There was a recurring Dáil bar set-up and impersonations of prominent politicians: Charlie McCreevy, Michael Noonan, Mary O'Rourke, Mary Harney. There were scenes at home of Taoiseach Bertie Ahern and his partner Celia Larkin preceded by an opening sequence in the style of *Dallas*. There were mock rituals where Dessie O'Malley would recite PD platitudes as if biblical prophecies and the audience would respond 'in the national interest' as a litany. There was reference to current political issues and scandals, such as refugees and tribunals. It showed former taoiseach Charles Haughey in a 'big house' type of prison. It reconstructed the Dáil chamber and the ceann comhairle disciplining deputies as if they were schoolchildren:

> — Deputy, what did the minister just say?
> — Do you want me to send you to the taoiseach's office?
> — Right, I'm putting you beside Tony Gregory for the rest of the day.

13 Interview with David Blake-Knox, 23 August 2001.

It went for media presenters and programmes too. Paddy O'Gorman was Paddy O'Gormless. *Prime Time* was *Slime Time*. Clare McKeon's talk show was called *The Clare Witch Project* and she was shown putting down her guests and exalting her own opinions and experiences. *Fair City* going to four nights a week was reduced to endless scenes of 'Cup of tea, Niamh?' There were jabs at business too. *Junket City*: 'all the time in the private sector; limited openings in the public sector'. On online banking: 'Why wait in line when you can wait online ... You save us the cost of employing a teller while you pay for the call.' There were swipes at many professions as well as popular clichés:

> — As they say, location, location, location.
> — Who says that?
> — People who say location a lot.

When the new computer system was introduced to the gardaí, a guard using a laptop immediately went to look up websites for *The Bill* and *Cagney and Lacey* and then sussed out programmes for keeping track of nixers and calculating overtime. The writing was uneven. It was funny, but often not funny enough. It was stronger on impersonation than satire. The humour was too gentle, more in the tradition of *Hall's Pictorial Weekly* than *Scrap Saturday*. There remains the need to take up the reins more assuredly from *Scrap Saturday* and to go for sharp satire, to live dangerously, to set the horns of the bull to charge at the tiger.

There was much stopping and starting in RTÉ drama through this period. The return of the single play slot didn't sustain itself. The sitcoms were not successful. The soap operas were all there was for long stretches and there were many problems with them. When presenting a paper at the *Imagining Ireland* conference at the Irish Film Centre in Temple Bar in 1993, I argued that RTÉ drama was in decline, that there was less drama than ever and what there was of it was tamer than ever.[14] There was a widespread sense that RTÉ was not delivering when it came to drama.

Two Lives
Two Lives was supposed to be a new start. It was 'to prove that RTÉ could do drama'.[15] The idea was basic: to commission a series of original half-hour plays by Irish writers according to a simple formula: each play would have two actors and one location. The project was to provide the audience with

---

14 Helena Sheehan, 'Soap Opera and Social Order: *Glenroe, Fair City* and Contemporary Ireland' – paper delivered at the *Imagining Ireland* conference at the Irish Film Centre, Dublin, 31 October 1993; also on the internet at www.comms.dcu.ie/sheehanh/itvsoap.htm. 15 A number of interviewees used this phrase when I asked about the production of *Two Lives*.

contemporary drama, to give Irish writers an opportunity to explore the medium of television, to make high quality drama on a low budget. The scheme was put to RTÉ by Michael Colgan of the Gate Theatre, who became the series producer. It was announced in 1993 that they planned to make 26 of them. As it turned out, there were 10.

The first three were aired in autumn 1993. *Tossed Salad* by Catherine Donnelly, an advertising copywriter, was an exploration of a Dublin 4 marriage in the wake of the revelation of an affair. The dialogue recognised that it was a cliché without quite rising above it. It seemed to attempt to puncture a veneer of sophistication to reveal ... what? Perhaps Dublin 4 paralysis at what to say of itself.

In High Germany by Dermot Bolger focussed on the changing nature of Irish identity in an era of cosmopolitan migration. Set in a Hamburg railway station and full of soccer references, a young man contemplated his past in Ireland and his future in Germany. The second life in this scenario, the girl-friend, only appeared at the end. It was basically a monologue on a particular view of nationhood and impending fatherhood.

Gold in the Streets by Thomas Kilroy set its sights on a father–daughter relationship, but it was also on the territory of emigration. An Irish father flew from Knock to find his daughter in a London squat. The conversations over several days constantly shifted in theme and tone through confrontations and confidences. The father reflected on changing times, on how farming was finished and now they made tea for German tourists, on much more besides: 'Nothing has prepared me for nowadays. Nowadays I never know what's coming next.'

Then there were another four in 1994. *A Mother's Love's a Blessing* by Pat McCabe was the most innovative and acclaimed of the series. It was a black comedy set on a farm about a mother-son relationship. It began:

> The world is a sad place, make no mistake. One minute you're happy as Larry and the next you're offered a machine gun to kill all around you. She was a desperate character, that mother of mine, but she used to make lovely sandwiches.

Pat, the son, not only spoke to his mother directly and compliantly, but behind her back defiantly: 'Yes, Detective Inspector Mammy.' He also played other characters he imagined, including one in full combat mode. Basically the plot was that of the smothering mother and the son coming of age and struggling to break free, especially when a different sort of interest in the opposite sex emerged. This was a particularly playful and ironic expression of the theme.

Seachange by John Banville was set on a pier in Dublin Bay. It was, until the end, a monologue of a loquacious man, who had lost his memory, who had returned to the place where he was found, his only link to his past, in the presence of a woman who remembered much, who was silent until the end, who had come to the place where her child had died.

Revenge by Anne Enright was set in Dublin, a rather Beckettian piece, which could have been subtitled 'suburbia, sex and videotape'.

Black and White by Kathy Gilfillan was set in London in an apartment of minimalist expensive elegance. An Irish woman, working in an art gallery, arrived to deliver a painting bought by the American woman who lived there. The Irish woman was fascinated by the sophisticated mystery of the other:

— Carol: What do you do?
— Marie Louise: I like nice things.

It was full of lesbian lure until the revelation of prostitution. It was ostensibly 'country girl coming to terms with cosmopolitan ways', but it was something other underneath it. The production itself exuded a smug self-regarding knowingness somehow, an indulgence of the idea of consuming without producing.

Boston Rose by Antoine Ó Flaharta concerned the interplay between an American *Rose of Tralee* contestant and her Irish escort. He was a trainee chef who wished he were a California surfer. She was looking for her Irish roots to his bemusement:

— She: Don't you want to know where you come from?
— He: I come from here.

The Celadon Cup by Hugh Leonard was set in a hotel in Istanbul and centred on an affair where the passion was turning to poison. At first it was bubbly chat and champagne, counterpointed by calls from Dublin. Although the message about the calls contained no message, the assumption was that it was the man's wife. If he were forced to choose between the woman or his wife, the woman made it clear that she was not his to choose. A tale was told of a cup changing colour when poison was put into it. She had seen poisonous relationships and had been taught that poison cured poison.

Then in March 1998 came the tenth drama: *Hell for Leather* by Roddy Doyle. This was part of an initiative to internationalise the idea and package the *Two Lives* productions with those made in other countries to the same formula and sell them abroad. In a Dublin kitchen, two women who met at the funeral of a Catholic priest explored their relationships with Father Brendan.

One was a Catholic working-class mother of three whose husband deserted her 'for a slut nearly twice his age'. The other was a single Protestant career woman. The Catholic woman, surprised at this, asked: 'Could you not find one of your own, a vicar or an ayatollah or whatever? It's like robbery.' As they compared notes on their mutual lover, an odd picture emerged. Wearing leather jackets and going to Springsteen and Eagles concerts was one thing, but shouting 'Good morning, Vietnam' at the moment of orgasm was quite another. It veered into *Father Ted* territory and went more for mockery than explanation or exploration. There was much scope for such mockery in the public mood after so many decades of betrayed reverence.

The reviews came in batches in 1993 and 1994. They were favourably received, some more than others, with the McCabe one most praised. None was panned, but they did fail to excite or provoke. I found them difficult to review in the way that some essays I get as a university teacher are difficult to mark. They are not bad, but they are not that good either, and it seems too callous just to write 'This is mediocre' on them. These plays were not stupid or clumsy or pointless, but they weren't stimulating, either. When each of them was over, I just didn't feel much of an impulse to say anything. When I went on television on the *Feedback* programme to review them in 1994, I said that they were disappointing. I did not think that the limitation of the form was the problem. I cited the Alan Bennett series *Talking Heads*, which had only one character in each, and simple sets, but the writing was insightful and ironic. They were stimulating and memorable. Michael Colgan, also on the programme, said that this was an invidious comparison, because some of the writers had written little more than a letter before (which raised the question of why they were commissioned to write for national television).

The only controversy coming out of these plays was within RTÉ. The producer-director grade in RTÉ protested against the use of a non-RTÉ, non-television series producer for an RTÉ in-house television series. They indicated that this was symptomatic of deeper problems in the development of new drama, pointing to the lack of a drama department or a coherent policy on drama and the discouragement of original ideas by RTÉ staff.[16] Liam Miller (director of television programmes at the time) responded that the proposal for the series came from Michael Colgan and must therefore be deemed to be his intellectual property. Addressing the broader question, he argued that drama departments were no longer the norm in broadcasting organisations and that the challenge to dated and costly work practices surrounding drama production had opened greater opportunities for drama experience.[17]

---

16 Statement of RTÉ producer-director grade, 10 December 1993. **17** RTÉ memo from Liam Miller to Michael Heney, 29 December 1993.

DRAMA DOCUMENTARY AND HISTORICAL DRAMA

Thou Shalt Not Kill

Making a more lasting impression were two series of drama documentaries on murders in Ireland under the series title *Thou Shalt Not Kill*. There were fifteen cases of murder covered in these series in 1994 and 1995 presented by Cathal O'Shannon and produced by Paul Cusack. The idea was for each programme to deal not only with the immediate circumstances of a murder, but to show what society was like in a particular part of Ireland at a particular time. They spanned a spectrum from *The True Story of the Colleen Bawn* from 1816, giving new treatment to an old legend, to *Murder in the Park*, still fresh in popular memory from 1982. The narrative of each case unfolded in a simple but rivetting manner. The story was told as O'Shannon recounted events, sometimes appearing on sites where events happened and sometimes as voice-over while monochrome dramatisations acted out events. There were also interviews intercutting these elements and telling crucial parts of the story. At the end, there were sometimes interesting footnotes to the story telling of subsequent developments.

The Green Tureen, for example, was the story of the murder of Hazel Mullen by Shan Mohangi, an Indian South African student studying at the College of Surgeons, in Dublin in 1963. He strangled her in a fit of possessiveness, cut up her body and attempted to burn it. For days he was searching for her with her distraught family. He was found guilty of murder and sentenced to death. On appeal, it was changed to manslaughter and he was given a sentence of seven years, of which he served three. He was deported to South Africa and elected an MP for the National Party. He was not re-elected in 1994, but continued in a comfortable life with a wife and three children, managing the family sugar plantation in Natal. He was interviewed and it was eerie to see him living and thriving while Hazel Mullen was long dead. These series made a lasting impression, much more so than the many glossily produced fictional murders that filled television screens every night of the week.

Most of the historical drama was done in co-production, although there were a few RTÉ in-house productions in this area, often done for anniversaries. *The Officer from France*, for example, showed the last days of Wolfe Tone, as part of RTÉ's commemoration of 1798 in 1998. There was also *The Battle of Kinsale*, which was made according to an implicit philosophy of history that is basically history with the people left out (or the overwhelming majority of them in the history of the world). It was low budget, which might have explained how whole battles were represented by two men in period costume jostling each other with sticks, but that did not justify the commentary in a drama documentary treating history as if made exclusively by aristocrats, whether they be English or Spanish monarchs or Gaelic chieftains.

MINI-SERIES, SERIALS AND CONTEMPORARY LIFE

Making the Cut

It had been a long time since RTÉ had made a detective series. The whole world was doing them after all, so why not Ireland? In fact, it had been a decade since RTÉ had done anything in the prime time one-hour serial format. The directive came, according to Niall Mathews, to do one, to make it contemporary and to set it in a city other than Dublin.[18] Perhaps too it was thought timely, as crime stories were particularly high-profile at the time with the murder of crime journalist Veronica Guerin in 1996. There were also questions being asked about how the forces of law and order had dealt with a history of transgressions by those in power in church and state coming forth like the eruption of a volcano. According to Diog O'Connell, 'It is no coincidence therefore that a police drama emerged from the rubble of all these stories, whether out of a need to imitate, explain, understand or simply express.'[19]

Making the Cut, based loosely on a novel by Jim Lusby of the same title, came forth as a two-hour pilot in October 1997 followed by four one-hour episodes. It was set in an unspecified Irish city played by Waterford. According to the *RTÉ Guide*:

> It tells a rough, tough and contemporary tale, stabbing into the underbelly of a world that has rarely been chronicled in an Irish drama series before … Gardaí based in a provincial town investigate a brutal crime which reveals a world where nothing is as it appears, a world peopled by the weak and vulnerable on the one hand and the greedy and venal on the other.

The *Guide* quoted producer Paul Cusack:

> The thread of these stories goes from the street right through society. From drug barons to the higher echelons of so-called respectable Irish society. This is another side of Ireland: one you won't find in the tourist brochures.[20]

---

18 Interview with Niall Mathews, 31 July 2001. Mathews was at the time head of drama and entertainment. The initiative came from Liam Miller who was director of television programmes. **19** Diog O'Connell, '*Making the Cut*', unpublished paper, 1997. **20** *RTÉ Guide*, 3 October 1997.

The plot opened in *film noir* style with a police operation involving drug dealing in a docklands location, where the arrest was botched. Then it moved to a closer look at the gardaí. Detective Sgt. Carl McCadden was a 'dirty harry' cop with a dark secret, an artsy loft and a history with other men's wives. He was partnered with Detective Moya O'Donnell, a quiet competent female new to this station. After initial difficulties, they developed a *modus operandi*. As the plot unfolded, various themes emerged: loner versus team player, sport for youth as antidote to crime, the cop who didn't get promotion going astray, the small fry criminal getting killed, while the big fish swims free.

In the serial following, investigation disclosed a scale of criminality rising to higher echelons of society. Driving from the provincial city to the capital, with the Financial Services Centre rising above the river, McCadden commented: 'The lair of the Celtic tiger. Dealers and chancers, the lot of them.' After questioning an executive of a construction company in a high rise office, McCadden moved into a high speed car chase and dragged a guy from a car and punched him without explaining to O'Donnell. She became motivated to look into his past and his involvement with a suspect on a case involving drugs, money laundering, insurance fraud and murder. This case four years earlier in Dublin was set out in flashback. In a moral dilemma between shielding his lover and doing his job, he chose the former. In the next episodes, O'Donnell in her turn was faced with such a choice: her heroin addict brother or her duty as a detective. She too chose the former. Both had crossed the line, but those they had set out to protect were still killed.

As the narrative moved to dénouement, a conspiracy between players in drug dealing, property development, telecommunications, law and politics was disclosed. In the face of a very corrupt society, the gardaí were nearly helpless. They primed a journalist with what they knew but could not prove and the journalist exposed the politician in line to become the next Minister for Telecommunications and Technology at a press conference. He was then arrested by the gardaí on election day. RTÉ news pondered the impact of revelations of corruption on the electorate. In the final scene, several weeks later, the new Minister for Telecommunications and Technology appeared on RTÉ affirming the integrity of Irish politics. When he left and got into his car, the same advisor who had been manipulating the interface between the legal face of power and its shadowy underbelly was revealed. Good did not triumph and evil carried on as the credits came up over the bright lights of Dublin and the shimmering waters of the Liffey.

Most reviews came after the pilot rather than after the whole six hours. It was generally thought to be a competent production of an international genre but with nothing specific enough to make it memorable. This was my own view of it as well. Some considered it to be imitative and mid-genre, because it was made more with an eye to international sales than to communicate with its domestic audience. Eddie Holt in the *Irish Times* called it the 'McDonaldisation of TV drama'. It proved, he said, that RTÉ could make a Big Mac with the best of them, but it was cop opera in a mode of television production dominated by accountants, where Irishness was subsumed to genre clichés, which blandified the narrative and pushed it perilously close to parody. He raised questions about the loner detective living in a loft in an urban wasteland, meeting an informer in a boxing gym and a string of stereotypes more suggestive of New York or London than Waterford. Against the stereotype, however, the sexual chemistry between the two leading crime fighters was mercifully understated. Summing it up:

> Their 1990s Ireland … is a country in which Mr Big (a corrupt businessman) can be exposed and still walk free. It is a country in which trickle down corruption ends in violence in poor council estates, where brutalised lumpen thugs brutalise all around them. It is a country where computer comfortable cops want a result and the worst of them are bent. It is, in short, not too wide of the mark and yet it is not *quite* Ireland.[21]

Coming back to it after the final episode (which critics rarely do), he focused on how figures such as Flanagan, the bullying bad ass, were put in perspective:

> As the visible underbelly of the tiger, Flanagan types receive huge media attention and, as a result of sometimes brave, but more often idiotic journalism, enjoy a weird kind of celebrity in this country. That there are greater forces – political, social and economic – propping up these assholes often goes unreported. At least this drama series got that much right and that is a lot.[22]

That much had to be said for *Making the Cut*. It did point to something in the character of the social order on a number of interlocking levels and not just individual goodies and baddies. However, it was vague about the nature of the problem. It seemed to be saying that crime and corruption were pervasive. Governments could come and go, certainly a particular politician's career could take a tumble, but the same people would be pulling the strings and the same thing would go on. It did not give a satisfactory sense, though, of who was in power and how and why.

---

21 Eddie Holt, *Irish Times*, 2 October 1997.　**22** Eddie Holt, *Irish Times*, 11 November 1997.

Making the Cut was followed in 1999 by another four-part series called *DDU* (District Detective Unit). The plots involved attacks on prostitutes, murder of a male prostitute, blackmail, drugs, a body in a bog and a container of Romanian refugees dumped at the docks. The scriptwriters for both productions, John Brown and Eric Deacon for *Making the Cut* and Michael Russell for *DDU*, were British, their previous credits including *Morse*, *Prime Suspect*, *Between the Lines* and *A Touch of Frost*, and the writing lacked fine tuning and a sense of specificity of Irish society.

Perhaps mid-genre stereotypical generality represented the conventional assumptions of television executives who did the buying and selling on the international market, but I would contest that this is what is necessary for drama produced in one country to play well in another. I believe that a well constructed narrative more firmly grounded in its time and place can communicate effectively across national boundaries. In any case, RTÉ found it more difficult to sell abroad than it expected, although I did notice its presence in the TV schedules in South Africa when I was there in 2001.

These experiments came and went, but the only consistent drama production in RTÉ during this period was in its long-running serials or soap operas.

Glenroe

Glenroe carried on through the 1990s in much the same way as it did in the 1980s. It wasn't that a lot of things didn't happen. There were births, deaths, marriages, affairs, disputes, crimes, businesses, projects galore. A stream of long-lost relations (remember Uncle Peter?) arrived and disappeared again. There were an extraordinary number of property transactions. There was much indulgent wheeling and dealing over farms, shops, restaurants, leisure centres, even gravel pits.

'Thou shalt not commit adultery' was still one of the ten commandments, but you would hardly guess it from the goings on in the byways and bedrooms of Glenroe. After teasing and testing the audience a few years before with the suggestion that Miley was the father of Davy O'Hagan (who arrived in Glenroe with Carmel from England), even Miley, would you believe it, eventually had a roll in the hay with Biddy's cousin Fidelma. Affairs, both licit and illicit, multiplied beyond memory: Dick and Terry, Dick and Venetia, Dick and Jennifer, even Dick and Mary again, on and on. Every character was paired at one time or other with a succession of others of the opposite sex, on the spectrum of passing fancy (Sgt. Roche and Shirley) to 'till death do us part' (Dinny and Teasy). There was everything else in between, including rape (Froggie and Bernadette), teenage pregnancy (Joseph and Catherine), faked pregnancy (Dan and Jennifer) and the most unlikely pairings (Blackie and Carol). The combining and recombining was confined to heterosexual attractions, however.

'Thou shalt not kill' was still the law of church and state, but that didn't stop Ray O'Driscoll from killing his brother Oliver. Transgression was ever the stuff of drama. Only certain kinds of transgressions could be explored, however. Murder, rape, burglary, deceit and non-marital sex (as long as it was heterosexual) could enter *Glenroe*, but homosexuality, atheism or a critique of class structure could not.

Yet with all the sex and deals and gossip going on, it still seemed to much of Ireland that not much was happening in *Glenroe*. It seemed too cosily cut off from anything outside itself. The world historical events preoccupying me in the late 80s and early 90s and causing the map of the world to be redrawn were registered in *Glenroe* only in the adoption of a Romanian child by George and Shirley Manning. However, in its own way it did register many of the changes in Irish society over the years. It did push out the boundaries in terms of sexual behaviour as the years went on. It did in many respects show a society where lifestyles were more various and attitudes were more diverse, but it did so in a low-intensity, perhaps even a lazy, way.

For example, the role of religion changed dramatically in Irish society in these years, while it changed rather undramatically in this drama. There were times when it was written with a bit of spark. Father Tim Devereux was a traditional priest who found it difficult to come to terms with newer trends, whether in the church or outside it. The best scenes were those where this was written with sensitivity to both sides of this tension. There were some scripts in 1988 written by Patrick Gilligan (of *The Spike*) where the priest reflected on how the power of the priest was not what it used to be and he tried to find his way into newer approaches. He engaged in discussions of liberation theology and liturgical dancing. He considered the position of those who were reading *Pedagogy of the Oppressed* and insisting that the church should be on the side of the poor. He said that the rich needed to be saved as well. Then his character would be written by someone else and it would all be forgotten. He was often caught up with greyhound racing. The dogs did sometimes have cute names like 'Bishop of Cork' and 'Minister for Arts, Culture and the Gaeltacht'. He was visited by a long-lost girl friend and assured her that his vocation had nothing to do with the fate of their romance. She died and left him a substantial amount of money in yet another *Glenroe* windfall.

The laicisation of a priest would seem to be a story charged with dramatic potential, yet the handling of the decision of Tim Devereux to leave the priesthood, despite having been solemnly ordained with the words 'Thou art a priest forever', was underwhelming, to put it mildly. Why did he do it? The scriptwriters didn't seem to know or care. It could have been the bank manager deciding to take early retirement. After saying that he intended to serve the community in another way, what did he decide to do? To be a piano tuner. When this proved not to be a viable proposition, he briefly went on the dole. He was then offered a job as a greenkeeper on Stephen Brennan's golf course. He moved in with Stephen, as Stephen's family had long been written out, in an 'odd couple' scenario, which had its amusing moments. He then had a vague kind of relationship with Shirley, who was widowed after George went off on an expedition to Peru in search of the habitat of the giant condor and was captured by a drug-dealing criminal gang. Shirley then invited Tim to go on a cruise she won in a raffle, provoking Stephen's jealousy. He then moved in with Michelle as a lodger and started writing a novel. Michelle found the novel called *Late Flowering*, a fictionalised account of the goings on in Glenroe over the years, and Venetia read from it at the Bard of Glenroe contest. This caused Father Tracey to accuse him of breaking the seal of the confessional.

The relationship between the new parish priest and the old one was interesting, although much more could have been done with it. It would have been highly unusual for a laicised priest to stay around in a parish where he had been stationed as a priest. However, it could happen. The spikey relationship between the two priests, despite its dramatic potential, was usually written superficially and played for easy laughs, rather than deeper contradictions and ironies. The new parish priest, Father Tracey, was also a very traditional priest in many ways, but very trendy and adventurous in other ways. He was theologically conservative and always wore clerical garb, but was keen to engage in new forms of evangelical activity. He could send text messages on a mobile phone. He was not the sharpest or most sensitive, but he was bubbling with enthusiasm. He was far more an activist than his predecessor had been in organising everything from stations to historical pageants. He asked Miley to be a minister of the eucharist and Denise to be an altar girl, but did not hit it off with Biddy.

Biddy, who had seemed all along the standard-issue *à la carte* Catholic, suddenly in 1996 had a crisis of faith. Why? What set it off? What did she think now about the questions to which Catholicism once provided the answers? Again, the scriptwriters didn't seem to have considered it very carefully. Not much was done with this story, which was part of the pattern: to avoid anything controversial or complicated most of the time, to occasionally raise something more difficult, but to deal with it superficially and then drop it. Biddy didn't go to meetings for Denise's first communion, said it was too much fuss and expense, then bought her a second-hand dress. She objected to having a station mass in her home, then conceded and turned up on the night. When Marianne recovered from meningitis, Biddy credited medical science, while Miley put it down to the power of prayer. She went to Christmas mass, albeit with a bit of a sulk, and there the story more or less ended. Biddy got on with domestic and agricultural matters, and nothing much was said about religion one way or the other. Biddy died in a car crash in April 2000. There was no funeral. This was not only undramatic, but dodged the issue of liturgical rites for someone who had ceased to believe. If there had been a funeral, it probably would have been done as it often is in real life where everyone ignores the problem and the person is buried in the same way as the true believer.

The priest and ex-priest continued to interact. They worked on a pageant to commemorate 1798 in the local area and on FÁS projects[23] to celebrate the millennium. They disagreed about what was the proper date to mark the millennium. Eventually Tim took up with the sister of his successor. The priest registered his discomfort, but came around by the final episode when he officiated at their wedding. Tim and Gracie worked together on the parish bulletin, which was revamped to become *Glenroe Hello*. Tim's impulse to do something like an interview with Stephen on how Vatican II had impacted on his life didn't quite work out and they went the direction of *Hello* magazine with a cover feature complete with photo spread on the life style of the Crosby-Morans in the big house giving soft-focus treatment to Venetia's absurd aristocratic pretensions. Father Tracey thought that it was a disgrace. However, the people of the parish received it well and so did the bishop. Here was a real clash of values between the old and new Ireland, even between different versions of the new Ireland, if anyone wanted to say anything meaningful about it. This lighthearted embrace of yuppie values flew in the face not only of the faith of our fathers but the liberation theology of many believers as well as the progressive views of many unbelievers. There were dramatic possibilities in this, but instead it was written with a kind of smug cuteness, which failed to deal with every issue it raised. It patronised its audience where it could have articulated contrary views, so that different sections of its audience would feel that their views were represented and stimulated in the dramatic interaction. Instead, it reverted to a tendency to blandify everything it touched, so as not to risk offending anyone. It could have given strong voice to diverging world views and conflicting moral values, which did exist even in rural Ireland, instead of creating a flat and false comfort zone, which it imagined its audience needed and wanted.

In an academic critique, Eoin Devereux characterised this tendency in *Glenroe* as 'theatre of reassurance'. He was concerned with how the *Glenroe* audience was constructed by those involved in its production and the implications of this for how it dealt with social problems, particularly poverty. He found in his interviews with those making *Glenroe* that they made assumptions

---

23 F[oras] Á[iseanna] S[aothair] : a state agency responsible for training and employment programmes, established in 1988.

about the programme, i.e., that it was entertaining and non-ideological, and about its audience, i.e., that it was a monolith and that they knew what it wanted. All of these assumptions, he argued, were questionable. He cited Barbara O'Connor's audience research against such assumptions about the audience. Younger viewers, she found, thought that the programme was light-weight and criticised its inattention to social problems.[24] He quoted one scriptwriter as saying that the programme should only reflect reality 'at a safe distance'. He asked the programme's creator about the poor: Wesley Burrowes answered that it was not the role of the programme to pontificate to them but to entertain them, to give them a world into which they could escape once a week where everything was predictable. Devereux argued that, in its refusal to acknowledge the existence of an unequal social structure and in the circumscribed way it dealt with stories touching on poverty, it was patently ideological. It was ideological because it treated inequality as taken for granted, which contributed to the reification of poverty and amounted to a refusal to challenge the basis of it or to show alternatives to it.[25]

'Blessed are the poor, for they shall be patronised with soap opera' might be one way of paraphrasing this attitude, but it only arose when being pushed on the question of poverty. The more predominant response I found, when-ever I raised questions about how society was constructed in the serial in my own interviews and informal interactions (from 1985 to 2001) with those involved in the production of *Glenroe*, was that it was not the role of the pro-gramme to deal with social issues. There was a growing defensiveness about social issues. My own critique of the programme in my book on Irish televi-sion drama in 1987, in my paper on soap opera and social order at the *Imagining Ireland* conference in 1993 and in various television programmes about the state of television drama, contributed to this atmosphere. Those involved argued over and over that the role of the programme was to enter-tain, end of story. The serial was about people and their relationships. However, if issues arose out of characters and their interactions, they inevitably said, they would deal with them. However, this begged all the ques-tions, I argued again and again, such as what people found entertaining and why. It evaded dealing with the fact that the whole thing was their construc-tion. The characters and their interaction were their constructions. The whole scenario could be constructed in such a way as to be either expansive or

24 Barbara O'Connor, *Soap and Sensibility: Audience Response to Dallas and Glenroe* (Dublin: RTÉ, 1990).
25 Eoin Devereux, 'The Theatre of Reassurance: *Glenroe*, its audience and the coverage of social prob-lems' in Mary Kelly and Barbara O'Connor, eds., *Media Audiences in Ireland* (Dublin: UCD Press, 1997). His study of *Glenroe* was part of a larger study of RTÉ in relation to poverty: Eoin Devereux, *Devils and Angels: the ideological construction of poverty stories on RTÉ* (Luton: University of Luton Press, 1998 [PhD thesis, Dublin City University, 1996]).

myopic in its relation to the social order. It could either look outward at the world in tune with relevant rhythms in the lives of interesting characters living interesting lives or it could be turned in on the trivial details of characters who live in cosy claustrophobia (and doing so without insight into the cosiness and claustrophobia).

Moreover, even on their own terms, they did not face up to issues that arose even in relation to their own characters and stories and the way they constructed them. I have given examples of such storylines to do with Tim Devereux and Biddy Byrne. I could multiply examples. Chuck and the rest of the Boyle family from Bray were brought in supposedly to represent the working class, the people of no property, those who had only their labour power and no ownership of the means of production. Within a few years, Chuck was no longer working on the Byrne farm, but came back from Australia as an entrepreneur, set up a business in Glenroe and even employed Dick Moran. The younger Boyles all became yuppies. There was a relentless preoccupation with people of property and their point of view. Those on other ends of the social spectrum, the occupants of the big house and the travellers, were written with a light touch. Class was never addressed with much honesty.

This defensiveness was demonstrated in a 1997 programme on RTÉ cele- brating fifteen years of *Glenroe*. It featured scenes from the show over the years interspersed with interviews with various people involved in its produc- tion, particularly Wesley Burrowes and various actors. The only academic or media critics to appear were ones who expressed unqualified approval. Not content with oozing adulation, the programme had several swipes at absent caricatured critics. John Waters said that Wesley Burrowes was a national treasure. Waters declared that, if *Glenroe* did what its critics wanted, it would be unwatchable. What its critics wanted was not represented in any way. There was another RTÉ programme hosted by Bryan Murray about soap operas and their appeal, populated entirely by actors and a studio audience. Actors from British and Irish soap operas were addressed as if they were their characters. It gushed with who fancied whom and wasn't it all great fun. It had a smothering effect. If you didn't have very strong self-belief, sitting at home watching, you would think that you must be crazy to be critical.

Glenroe, it must be said, had consistently high production values. There was always good acting and directing and sometimes good writing. It had high TAM ratings. It was never embarrassing. Its success shielded it from criticism. The attitude was: if it topped the TAMs, and it often did, what else needed to be said? The numbers showed that people were watching, but did not tell what they were thinking. I rarely missed an episode in its whole run, but there was an attitude that anyone like me didn't count. It was being made for an audi- ence conceived of as older, rural and conservative, by people who were mostly middle aged, urban and liberal. They did sometimes try to push at the limits they imagined that RTÉ was imposing on them,[26] but this tended to be too focused on seeing how far they could go in the area of sexual transgression, rather than on dramatising class inequalities, questioning received religion, or representing the clash of world views playing themselves out in contemporary Ireland. On the 1997 programme on fifteen years of *Glenroe*, Luke Gibbons said that, if you wanted to show someone from Mars what Ireland was like in these years, you couldn't do better than to show them *Glenroe*. However, not even those making it claimed, at least when pressed, that it was a realistic portrayal of contemporary Ireland.

In January 2001 RTÉ announced that *Glenroe* would end its eighteen-year run in May. Cathal Goan, director of television, summoned cast and crew and thanked them for their contribution to making 'one of the most loved and watched series ever produced by RTÉ', but declared that it had come to a natural end and would not be renewed after its current run. In an interview with me, he addressed it on another level. It was a whimsy, he said. Whatever it was, it was not contemporary Ireland. They had done a lot of soul-searching about it and considered a number of solutions, but decided that a process had brought it to a place from which it couldn't escape.[27] Various actors were interviewed in the media, including a number of them together on *The Late Late Show*. They regretted its ending, believed RTÉ should have put more resources into it and kept it going, but basically they took it on the chin and continued to work on the final episodes.

In the final episode, Miley Byrne went back to Bracken and visited Biddy's grave in Glenroe and discussed with his daughters the possibility of selling eggs on the internet before gathering with other characters and extras for the wedding of their former parish priest. It did register the changes in its way.

The *RTÉ Guide*, which once upon a time had articles with some kind of analysis of television, had pages and pages of pictures commemorating the show. It told the whole origin myth again: in the beginning was *The Riordans*.[28] It had features on the births and marriages, on Dick's women and on collected 'infidelities'.[29] It didn't get off so easily with the newspaper critics. Diarmuid Doyle's article in the *Sunday Tribune* addressed the decision to axe the show. In an article entitled 'Glenroe goes the way of the Dodo, like rural Ireland', he

---

26 In response to an audience research report on *Glenroe* produced by Lansdowne Market Research in May 1995, producer Tom McArdle tried to get more young characters and more characters per episode (internal RTÉ memo, 22 June 1995) to which Liam Miller responded that doing what would appeal to younger viewers would provoke hostile reaction from its core audience (internal RTÉ memo, 29 June 1995). **27** Interview with Cathal Goan, 29 August 2001. **28** H. Sheehan, *Irish Television Drama*, pp. 128–35, 158–62, 182–3, 342–60. **29** *RTÉ Guide*, 4 May 2001.

berated the serial for playing safe and steering clear of anything resembling the reality of rural Ireland.[30] John Boland's column in the *Irish Independent* was headed 'Glenroe dozing off into the sunset'. He lashed at the *RTÉ Guide* for 42 photographs plus mindless puffery instead of any analysis of what *Glenroe* once meant or was intended to mean as drama or sociology. Turning to the final episode:

> So you switched on the final episode to try to recapture something that would link you to those lost years when the world and *Glenroe* were younger – and *you* were younger too – but all you got were reminders of how *Glenroe* had long since failed as drama ... nothing at all has been happening in *Glenroe* – not just nothing with any relevance to the way we live now, but nothing whatsoever. And so it ended.[31]

It ended, but it must be evaluated in a way that those responsible for it failed to do, at least in public. It was good in many ways, but it could have been much better. It could have been more honest with itself and its audience about how we live now and about all our contrasting views of how we live now. The soap opera may be in its conventions a cosy and conservative form, with its origins in an extremely cosy and conservative society, but it is nevertheless a form that has enormous potential to open out and to show the structure of the social order and to probe the human psyche as it is shaped by the social order. There is so much time to develop character, so much scope to elaborate the twists and turns of storylines. Instead of fulfilling this potential, soap operas have tended to go round and round, recycling soap-opera clichés, endlessly pairing and triangulating, rather than venturing into this almost uncharted territory. *Glenroe* in any case did not venture there. As one RTÉ executive most astutely said to me, *'Glenroe* never missed an opportunity to miss an opportunity.'

Fair City
Fair City came into the world bearing an enormous burden of expectations. Since the demise of *Tolka Row*,[32] but accelerating in succeeding decades, there was a sense of a yawning gap in the picture of Irish society emerging from RTÉ drama. All through the 1980s there was talk of the need for an urban serial. Indeed, there was almost a sense of desperation about it, a sense that it must happen and that it must succeed. Its mandate was to be urban and contemporary and to be hard-hitting in tackling social issues. When RTÉ announced it in its autumn schedule for 1989, it was at the centre of anticipation, not only

30 Diarmuid Doyle, 'Glenroe goes the way of the Dodo, like rural Ireland', *Sunday Tribune*, 28 January 2001. **31** John Boland, 'Glenroe: dozing off into the sunset', *Irish Independent*, 12 May 2001. **32** H. Sheehan, *Irish Television Drama*, pp. 122–8.

from the media, but from the audience. Much effort and major investment had gone into its development. The documents in the archives refer to it as *Glasfin*, then as *Northsiders*, but by the time it appeared on the air, it was *Fair City*, from the song *Molly Malone:* 'In Dublin's fair city/ Where the girls are so pretty ...'

The opening sequence evoked Dublin, beginning with aerial shots of the city, inserting scenes of O'Connell bridge, the river, a park, a schoolyard, a betting shop, a pub, neighbours talking over hedges of corporation houses, finally homing in on the Drumcondra area, which was to be the fictional Carrigstown. The pilot opened with a succession of breakfast scenes in a number of houses with a running thread of various characters commenting on the story on the front of the *Northside People*, featuring the first anniversary of the Copeland House Community Enterprise Centre. As the day went on, these characters all converged on this centre. Throughout the day, there were scenes of Dublin as we knew it: Cumberland Street labour exchange (Paddy signing on), Grafton Street (Bernie on a rendezvous), Bewley's café (ex-lovers Bernie and Breffni meeting again) and Barry and Paul running in the park. In between there was much happening: people coming and going, phone messages being conveyed, characters gossiping about other characters, rows about relationships and about money. The pilot ended with a party at the centre which ended in a punch-up, because Paddy took exception to Paul kissing Anne (not knowing that Bernie had been kissing Breffni).

Following the pilot, there was a flurry of reviews. RTÉ even did a vox pop on the streets of Dublin. Most people said that they couldn't make out what was going on. Some complained about the accents, speaking in the same accents themselves. The consensus among the critics, of whom I was one, was that it had got off to a frenetic start, that it was not clear who was doing what and why, but that it was promising and should be given a chance. So many characters and situations were introduced so quickly that it was impossible to make much sense of it at first viewing. I couldn't keep track of who was related to whom and doing what, let alone why. I came home from the preview, read the potted biographies of the characters in the RTÉ publicity material and watched it again on transmission and it became a bit clearer.[33] Another critic said that, even with the benefit of the press pack and seeing it twice, the relationships remained abstruse.[34] Looking at it a third time, for the purposes of assessing the evolution of the serial, it looked very different with twelve years' knowledge of the subsequent history of the characters and storylines behind me, but it was what it looked like on the night that mattered.

The pace slowed somewhat, sometimes to the point of the pedestrian. All sorts of things were tried, but the audience fell and the critics became harsher.

---

33 Helena Sheehan, *New Nation* 8, 1989.   **34** Eddie Holt, *Irish Independent*, 23 September 1989.

Inside RTÉ, there was consternation, but also commitment to do whatever it took to fix it. Sometimes it seemed that the desperation to make it better only made it worse. It was trying too hard to be something without being too sure what that something was. It was too bitty. There was too much happening for too little reason. It was too imitative. It was looking too much to *EastEnders* and not enough to contemporary Dublin.

By the end of the first series, the centre was burnt down. Tony, the long lost son of Mags and Charlie Kelly, had returned and discovered that Robert Copeland was his father. Copeland arrived to settle the insurance claim and proposed marriage to Bernie, daughter of Mags and sister of Tony. Meanwhile characters had to find alternative employment. All through the series there was much pairing and triangulating, starting with Paul and Bernie, Bernie and Breffni, Paul and Anne, but many more too. TV critic Eddie Holt wondered if *Fair City* should be called *Affair City*.[35] In subsequent series the affairs multiplied. Bela returned from womanising in London to womanising in Dublin. He had hardly settled back to home and hearth with Rita when he had an affair with Linda, who had a baby, and then married Barry. Then Bela took up with Cliodna, separated again from Rita and took up in succession with Irene, Tamara, Pauline, Gina and Tess. Anne took up with Paul, Jack, Frank, Shay, Liam, Dermot, Philip, Clancy, before going off to work on a cruise ship. As to Paul, who could remember all those between Bernie and Anne in the early days and Helen and Nicola and Niamh in more recent years?

There was wheeling and dealing, much of it revolving around Jack Flynn, the local shady entrepreneur, and subsequently around Éamonn Clancy, who also disappeared eventually, leaving a string of bad debts behind him, and latterly by Dermot Fahy and Seán Mc Cann, local politicians as well as businessmen. An extraordinary numbers of characters have owned their own local businesses: a recording studio, a coffee shop, a hair salon, a pizzeria, a pub, a bistro, a sandwich bar, a law firm, a computer business, a garage, a taxi operation, a health club, a painting contractor, a cleaning service, a classic corner shop, an accountancy practice, a dresser, not to mention the black economy operations: money-lending, drugs and prostitution. Although most characters were supposed to be of working class origins, hardly any of them have been wage labourers. Those that have been, have worked primarily in the local businesses. Hardly any have belonged to trade unions. Those who must have been, by the nature of their jobs, for example, teachers such as Barry or Andrew, weren't inclined to mention it.

There were comings and goings, births and deaths, windfalls and debts, rows and reconciliations, and so on, but there rarely seemed to be a sufficient

35 Ibid.

reason why. There were rapes, abortions, kidnappings, sexual harassment, blackmail, murder, but how dramatic any of it was depended utterly on how compelling was the characterisation of those involved, on how convincing was the motivation for the acts committed. It often seemed to be soap opera by numbers.

In the course of my research in 2001, I was amazed to discover memos dating as far back as 1990 and 1991 from David Blake-Knox, who was then head of the drama, variety and young people's departments at RTÉ, to the *Fair City* production team. These addressed the problems in the writing of *Fair City* in a forthright, perceptive, and sometimes devastating fashion.[36] He said that the writing was too often predictable and bland, the plot structures were too mechanical and the resolutions were too neat. Characterising the characters, he said:

> Put crudely, there are too many bland or dull characters in *Fair City*. They tend to be passive in their relation to events and to lack clear definition of their emotional needs and reflexes. Too often their actions seem dictated by the structural exigencies of the script and lacking in strong or wholly credible motivation.

And of their relationships:

> Overall, it seems to me that there is a sort of vacuum at the centre of almost all these relationships. They tend to lack depth and an internal dynamic – what we see on the surface is really all there is.

As to the storylines, in the first year, they were characterised by excessive melodrama and self-conscious addressing of social issues and then in the second year, by an over-reaction to this in a kind of dull naturalism. He wanted it to avoid both pitfalls. He also addressed the nature of the Carrigstown community:

> I still find a persistent stress upon the old notion of 'community'. It is almost as if last season's collection of individual claustrophobic family ménages had been replaced this season by one large claustrophobic extended family. Nobody appears to work outside its parameters; they all shop in the same place; they all drink in the same pub. Sounds more like a remote village in the west of Ireland than central Dublin. In any

---

36 David Blake-Knox, RTÉ internal memos to *Fair City* production team, 25 April , 14 and 16 August 1990, and 24 July and 4 November 1991.

case, the whole concept of working class community is very problematic for me – smacking as it does, of romantic condescension. At times, the picture which emerges in these scripts is of a pre-television society – living a communal life on the streets and in each other's pockets.

And over a year later:

> Confrontation, when it occurs, is almost entirely personal and lacking in any social resonance. This is one of the reasons that I think the series lacks a sense of place. Linda's pregnancy is also symptomatic of the failure to connect Carrigstown with a larger society. It is as if no public dimension is allowed to intrude into her private story. There is hardly a mention – even in passing – of hospitals, social welfare, or any other practicalities. In fact, there is very little evidence of this community being connected with any of the popular institutions of modern Ireland.

He argued that 'community' did not have to be seen as everyone living together and thinking the same thing. Sometimes conflict could define the parameters of community. The difference in class background between characters, such as Paul and Cliodna, could be explored to clarify the type of place Carrigstown was supposed to be. He emphasised that he was not advocating heavy-handed portrayal of class conflict, but that he thought that an awareness of this dimension could add dramatic perspective to storylines.

Whatever happened within the production process as a result of such a critique, it was not apparent to the viewer or critic watching the production. In autumn of 1993 when presenting my paper to the *Imagining Ireland* conference, it still seemed that the opening sequence evoked Dublin (I showed it on video), but I contended that Carrigstown did not feel to me like Dublin. It was more like a 1950s rural village than a 1990s city. Everybody lived in each other's pockets and knew each other's business. Nearly everybody worked in the immediate area. This was soap-opera convention, but it was not urban life. The only serial to break with this was *Brookside* in its early years, where characters lived in Brookside Close, but moved about and worked in the larger city of Liverpool in a way that worked and opened up new territory for the genre, even if it collapsed back into the genre convention in the ensuing years, with nearly everybody living and working in each other's pockets.

Those involved in the production of *Fair City*, to whom I spoke while writing that paper, answered that the budget did not allow for location shooting. I thought that *Fair City* should have been given the resources for location shooting (and if it was necessary to get rid of *The Rose of Tralee* to do so, so much the better). However, I did not believe than this alone would solve the problem, which was a problem of vision. Even without location shooting, dialogue could refer outward in a way that it rarely did. Characters could come and go from the larger city and they could read books and newspapers, listen to radio, watch television, communicate by fax and e-mail. In countless ways, they could be constructed in a conscious and dynamic relationship to the wider world. For most of the first five years of *Fair City*, characters came and went, consumed their pizzas and pints, did their deals, had their flirtations and affairs, their births, marriages, separations and deaths in a so-what sort of way, without sufficient rhyme or reason, or specific texture, or particular perception.

It was striking for me to discover years after that there were critiques so similar to this, even using certain turns of phrase, that had been made several years earlier by those with more power to shape the serial. Yet, despite the 1990–1 memos, it continued in the same mode enough for the same critique to be made by me in 1993 and for it to call forth a strong affirmative response in a number of people in the audience, including one who was centrally involved in the writing of *Fair City*. I did think that *Fair City* was improving. I cited storylines running at the time: Rita going back to school and doing her Leaving Cert., Bela adjusting to living in a flat out of Carrigstown, Barry's ideas about running the school, Natalie planning to come back to work after her baby was born, not knowing that those who smiled and told her to take care were plotting against her. There were bits of dialogue giving it more texture: Natalie referring to her baby as 'yer wan kickin' away like Paul Mc Grath' and Lorraine wanting to stay in the room because it was 'all part of family interaction … we learned it in life skills class'.

Critiques, reports and new turns
All the same, I argued, *Fair City* and *Glenroe* needed to engage with the society in which they were set in more ways than this. Here were some questions I asked of those who made these programmes:

> What did Biddy and Bela think about the big issues of our times?
>
> Did anyone in Glenroe or Carrigstown have left- or right-wing views?
>
> Had anyone noticed that the map of the world had been redrawn?
>
> Did anyone notice that Ireland elected a feminist president?
>
> Did anyone vote?
>
> Were the residents of Glenroe and Carrigstown the only people in Ireland with no opinion on the *X* case?

Were they the only ones in the country not to make remarks about bishops and babies?

Was everyone a religious believer?

Would GATT agreements or structural funds allocation affect them?

Did anyone belong to a trade union?

Did no local TD ever come into Teasy's or Mc Coy's?

Did no one go to TCD, UCD, DCU or any 3rd level educational institution?

Did no one work at Intel or Unidare or Aer Lingus or any large industrial enterprise?

Why did such a disproportionate number of characters own small businesses and those few who worked for a wage work for them?

Was Clancy supposed to represent the whole capitalist system?

It was not, I stated, that any one of these absences was that conclusive, but taken together they indicated what I at least found missing, at least the surface of what I found missing. But, even staying on the surface, I indicated some characters I would like some day to see: a married laicised priest, a nun who lived in a flat after coming under the influence of liberation theology in Latin America, a trade union official, a government programme manager, a multinational executive, a computer hacker, a philosopher (why not?), a novelist, a journalism student, a night cleaner, a carpenter who could only find work in the black economy, a person who was long-term unemployed, a punter who voted PD and thought that the *Sunday Independent* was the fount of all wisdom, a communist whose life came into crisis in 1989.

Adding any such characters, I knew, would not solve the problem in itself, but written well they could open out the scenario to show the structure of the social order in terms of the rhythms of everyday lives. Some of these absences became presences in due course: both serials eventually had married laicised priests; Fidelma in *Glenroe* worked for Aer Lingus and Biddy even worked in a factory for a time; Eoghan and then Suzanne and Sarah in *Fair City* were university students and Fiachra was a university lecturer; politicians began to appear in McCoy's pub, as did a computer hacker and a multinational executive. As to the carpenter, construction was booming. Frank and Damien did painting and decorating and had plenty of work. Hannah was a school cleaner in between working behind the counter of one family shop and then another. Even trade unions got a mention in relation to teachers and 'all that time off with strikes'. Nevertheless, there was still much missing.

RTÉ commissioned audience research reports on *Fair City* in 1990, 1995 and 2001. The overall assessment of the 1995 report was seen to mark a significant improvement on the 1990 results. The audience was averaging 750,000 per episode. The face-to-face interviews of 1387 respondents at 70 sampling points were conducted by Lansdowne Market Research in February 1995. Bela Doyle and Hannah Finnegan were the most popular characters, while Eamon Clancy, Wayne Molloy and Nicola Prendergast were the least popular. The Anne Clarke–Éamonn Clancy affair was considered the top storyline, whereas stories to do with Lily being haunted by Mary's cat and Charlie breeding fish were least well received. They were asked what sort of stories they would like to see in the future from a multiple choices list: stories about older characters, stories about younger characters, social issues (specified as marital breakdown et cetera), romance, comedy, adult stories, glamour, crime, other (specify). The preference reported was for comedy and romance.[37]

The 2001 report conducted by Emer Hatherell Qualitative Research was based on eight focus groups in four locations. The key findings of the report included: soap operas fulfil a need for vicarious living; viewers enjoyed a more intimate relationship with the characters on *Coronation Street* than with those in *Fair City* as they 'are taken through all aspects of these characters' lives and journey through the labyrinths of their minds' (I kid you not); the most engaging storylines dealt with affairs and social and moral dilemmas. The characters were seen as too one-dimensional. The report stated that Helen came across as a tough businesswoman, but viewers were exposed to few other aspects of her character (presumably this was referring to Nicola, as Helen had been dead for two years and was not a businesswoman). The character of Eunice was seen as highly credible and evoked a very positive response in terms of both the writing and acting. The portrayal of the relationship between Kay and Malachy after her abortion received a negative assessment. The report offered suggestions for new storylines: Mike could have a one night stand with Jasmine, Floyd could lead Tara astray, Damien could get Suzanne pregnant, McCann could organise devious land rezoning and place the blame on Dermot. Additional characters they would like to see: 'a glamorous female, a man-eating woman, a good comic, a real bad boy'.[38]

My scepticism about the value of qualitative audience research was intensified by reading these reports. Far too much is concluded from far too little.

---

37 Lansdowne Market Research, *Fair City Assessment*, February 1995. **38** Emer Hatherell, *Fair City: A Qualitative Evaluation*, March 2001.

What respondents say to oral multiple-choice questions or in focus group scenarios is off the top of the head, selective and superficial. The samples are small. The crudity of the categories such as 'adult stories' and 'glamour' and equating social issues with marital breakdown cannot yield anything but crude results. Factual errors to do with the names of characters and length of time a series has been on air do not inspire confidence. The suggested characters and storylines are clichés.

Further, although it is obviously a matter of conflicting perceptions, I do not find the character of Eunice credible or interesting and find the acting style disruptive as it seems more appropriate to panto than to television. The portrayal of the relationship between Kay and Malachy, however, I believe, was subtle, credible and mature both in the way it was written and acted. As to who were the most or least popular characters, the answers indicate more what sort of people they might like to have for friends than what sort of characters make good drama. Taking such opinions seriously would produce only 'pollyanna' personalities and no dramatisation of human negativity or conflict.

Coming at *Fair City* in the context of a comparative study of soap operas and society in thirteen European countries in the 1990s, Scottish academic Hugh O'Donnell viewed these serials not as texts in themselves, but as sites of an ongoing process of negotiation between producers and consumers taking place within a larger framework. Describing soap operas:

> they have an almost organic existence as they squirm and coil their way forward unpredictably through time, moving this way and that as the range of pressures exerted on them vary in intensity, sometimes carrying their audiences with them, sometimes alienating them, sometimes expiring through fatigue or dying a spectacular death.[39]

O'Donnell argued that soap operas told their own story about their society at a level that transcended the factual detail of their individual storylines. This was part of a greater overarching narrative created simultaneously by all the soaps. Although competing ideologies were seldom explicated, he contended, this narrative unfolded within a Europe in which social democratic hegemony was on the defensive in the face of a neo-liberal onslaught. The tradition of public service broadcasting was challenged by the advance of new commercial channels and attitudes. He placed the soap operas he studied along a spectrum, with British soaps at one end as a refuge of the embattled social democratic world

---

39 Hugh O'Donnell, *Good Times, Bad Times: Soap Operas and Society in Western Europe* (London: Leicester University Press, 1999), p. 24.

view and the newer German ones at the other end as the realm of a young afflu-
ent depthless consumerist culture in the mode of *Neighbours* or *Dallas*. In
between the two extremes were all sorts of permutations, which was where he
placed *Fair City:*

> the unconvincing upward mobility of *Fair City* in Ireland, where the
> economic opportunities opened up by the tiger economy allow erst-
> while proles to open furniture-restoring workshops in lock-up.[40]

Fair City placed itself within the social-realist tradition of British soaps,
O'Donnell argued, but failed to deliver anything like the level of social
comment provided by its British counterparts. This, I would contend, over-
stated the level of social comment in the British ones and understated that of
Fair City. Although he cited my 1987 book on Irish television drama and my
1993 paper on soap operas in support of his negative evaluation of Irish television drama in general and *Fair City* in particular, I found myself on the defensive and inclined to argue that our soap operas should not be compared so
unfavourably with those of other European countries, particularly with those
of Britain, which I have also watched consistently. I do not think that watching
a few episodes of *Fair City* in 1994 and again in 1997 formed an adequate basis
for judging such a long-running serial. It is difficult to feel the force of the dis-
tinction he articulated as:

> Whereas in the British soaps working class experience is *dis*placed into
> petit bourgeois class positions, in *Fair City* working class experience is
> *re*placed by petit bourgeois aspirations.[41]

Explaining this in relation to *Brookside* and *EastEnders*, he said:

> the displacement of selected aspects of working class experience into
> (and the concomitant rejection of neo-liberal values from) the lives of
> petit bourgeois characters continues to be a defining feature ... the iso-
> lated, embattled and inward looking group of people who populate
> British soaps can be seen to represent the very real and widespread dis-
> array of the British working class ... political issues raised by soaps such
> as *Eastenders* and *Brookside* are constantly deflected and contained by
> being placed firmly within the framework of the family ... they are also
> structurally diffused by the atomised, fragmented and unorganised

---

40 Ibid. pp. 225–6.　**41** Ibid. p. 108.

class position of the protagonists. This is largely what gives British soaps their simultaneously progressive and conservative feel.[42]

And in relation to *Coronation Street*:

> *Coronation Street* is set in a Britain which never was and never will be, a country of publicans and shop owners where problems from the real world are taken in, reworked and reconfigured: they are transformed from political issues to personal ones and dispersed into an unending flow of narrative.[43]

As to *Fair City*:

> It constructs, even if only by default (which is … what hegemony is about), the new neo-liberal consensus of classless individuals moving up the ladder of personal wealth (though never very far) thanks to their own individual endeavours. The real (and very obvious) imbalances of Ireland's tiger economy in the 1990s are nowhere to be seen. Economic power is everywhere in microscopic amounts in *Fair City*, but nowhere in substance: it is a placeless utopia, neither rural nor urban, but combining elements of the mythologies of both.[44]

There was much in these assessments, but they were nevertheless not quite on the mark with respect to *Fair City*. It was initiated and sustained within the tradition of public service broadcasting and it came from an impulse to give dramatic expression to the realities of contemporary Irish society. It might have done so inadequately and given too much ground to genre clichés, but it has not given unequivocal expression to neo-liberal individualism either. It has reflected commercial pressures and individualist values, but not unequivocally, not unquestioningly, not alone in the dramatic frame.

Fair City has felt the pressure of all ideological currents in Irish society to an extent not always obvious in the text itself. A *Nighthawks* sketch in 1991 showed a top RTÉ executive being asked by a journalist: 'Do you think that *Fair City* is marxist enough?' to which he answered that they had better work on that. Those in the know knew that it was a reference (and a funny one) to alleged Workers Party influence in RTÉ (which has been much exaggerated). What has prevailed in *Fair City* has been a liberal social democratic point of view, no longer under strong pressure from the old right or new left and confused by the nature of the challenge from the new right. Not that those

---

42 Ibid. p. 210.   **43** Ibid.   **44** Ibid. p. 109.

involved in its production would customarily speak or even think about the production in such explicit ideological terms. It has given expression, implicitly or explicitly, to neo-liberal attitudes, in some characters and situations, but it has not constructed a neo-liberal consensus of classless individuals.

As the years moved on, *Fair City* evolved. By 2001 it was going out 4 nights a week with 30 writers, a large and efficient production team and an average audience of 650,000. By January 2002 it had aired over 1000 episodes. The new opening sequence made in 1997 was a stylish evocation of the city: panning over the Pigeon House at dawn, the distillery, an older city street, people walking along the strand by Dublin Bay, the fruit stalls and bustle of Moore Street, O'Connell Street, the bridges over the shimmering River Liffey at dusk. It was the look of a city that had come up in the world, as indeed it had. It was the time of the tiger. It showed too in the look of the sets and lives of the characters. They were less downtrodden, but they were not fabulously rich with unearned wealth either. Most of them were working class in origin and had achieved a modestly comfortable standard of living through education and work and presumably through the rising tide lifting many (if not all) boats. There were still too many of them who owned and worked in local businesses.

It had more of a feel of the city about it. There was more of a sense of the larger city. Some of the characters (Nicola, Paul and Niamh) had flats outside Carrigstown, but came there to work. Malachy went off to a homeless shelter to work. Suzanne and Sarah went to university. There was some location shooting in shopping centres, night clubs, city streets. Also the outdoor set built on an RTÉ lot with house and shop fronts, streets and bus stop as well as the studio sets for pub, bistro, shops, flats and offices had an authentic look of contemporary Dublin about them. There was also more of a sense of the wider world in the way the script referred outward, even when the cameras didn't go there. It was intermittent and it varied with scriptwriters. One character, for example, would mention Eskimos, while another came in saying that the correct term was Inuits, to which the other replied: 'Are you going to call Amnesty International?'

There was in the earlier years a 'no politics, no religion' rule,[45] but this was no longer in force. There was still a certain caution in dealing with politics. The politics of the north was an area that was avoided. The notion of politics running through the serial was quite vague, but occasionally something vivid broke through. There were eventually politicians who were regular characters. Seán McCann and Dermot Fahy were local councillors and businessmen who belonged to 'the party'. Although the party was never named, it was

---

45 Interview with Kevin McHugh, 29 August 2001.

unmistakably Fianna Fáil. There were references, even if only in passing, to the tribunals and the political corruption exposed in them. McCann was in time discovered by Fahy to have been implicated in the corrupt practices that had been routine in his time in the party. A deal was made and he resigned and left Carrigstown and the series, rather than be publicly exposed (which would have been much more interesting). There were even mentions of actual politicians and events, such as one character telling another that if he went to prison, it wouldn't be to Liam Lawlor's cell.[46]

Sometimes there were storylines that situated the local community and its characters in relation to power and property. One was about the closure of the local library, basically about public property and who had control of it. There was a romantic connection between Dermot and Jo, a politically articulate woman who led the opposition to the party on this issue, but the relationship could not develop because of their different politics. She went off to Athlone, then came back to Dublin again and they had another go. They again found themselves on the opposite sides of political issues, however vaguely sketched these issues were.

Another instance was a local pirate radio station, which Dermot had closed down by the gardaí, after Charlie Kelly, feeling a sense of power as a local broadcaster, started giving out about certain politicians and naming him. Charlie went into oppositional overdrive and started citing Marx and Engels and the *Communist Manifesto*. He sat down with his pint in McCoy's and explained that state power equalled violence. When the gardaí arrived to close the station, Eunice Phelan was on air with some new agey nonsense and started singing 'We Shall Overcome'. It stretched credibility (for me at least) to believe that she was the sort of person who would sing 'We Shall Overcome', but I was happy that some scriptwriter still remembered it. When the incident was reported on the front page of the *Northside People*, she got on her galloping high horse about paparazzi and 'the sort of people who killed Princess Diana', which seemed more ideologically in character. When they came to court, the judge told Charlie that one Éamon Dunphy in Ireland was enough, to which Charlie took exception, saying that he had modelled himself on John Bowman: 'scholarly, measured, well researched, impeccably presented'.

Another struggle was a rent strike and eviction involving private property. Tara McCann, sharing a flat with other 20-somethings Jasmine, Jason and Jerry, worked for a (vague) charity and spoke of power and wealth and inequality in a radical way. Even when 'going girly' in an effort to attract Jimmy

---

46 Liam Lawlor was a Fianna Fáil TD who was imprisoned for non-compliance with the requirements of a tribunal of inquiry into payments to politicians.

Doyle, prompting Jerry to remark: 'So there's a little Claudia Schiffer inside the Che Guevara' she wondered if the £25 frilly top she bought was made in a sweatshop where workers got paid 25p. However, it was not clear how deep her politics went and how much of it was sublimation of oedipal tensions with her father. The politician and landlord was her father. Another of her causes was animal rights, but her activity here was also related to her father's financial and sexual ties.

An important story reflecting the evolving relationship of Ireland to the politics of the wider world was the entry of a refugee into Carrigstown. Ashti was a Kurdish teacher who fled to Ireland, feeling caught between the Turkish authorities and those in armed struggle against them. At first, the only work he could find was selling the *Big Issue* on the streets of Dublin. Then he came to work in Phelan's shop, and Eunice, going through a regression therapy phase, imagined that he was the reincarnation of a husband she had in a previous life, and Christy began to see his inheritance diverted. Eunice denounced her son as racist on Radio Carrigstown. I think that it was a mistake to tie the refugee story to reincarnation fantasies. It was also marred by discordant acting styles, which weakened its impact. Nevertheless, it did highlight the difficult lives asylum seekers left behind, in this case including torture, the ruthlessness of those who profiteered on their transit and the suspicions surrounding them on arrival.

Carrigstown slowly became slightly multi-racial. Black extras began to sit up at the bar in McCoy's pub. A black woman named Venus O'Brien was a vixen who seduced Brian Maher away from lovestruck Farrah Phelan. The actress complained about the role and her treatment by the show. In 2002 an African doctor arrived, set up as a GP in the area and took up with Nicola. Arriving to find that he had been with her daughter overnight, Nicola's mother made it clear that she did not find inter-racial sex acceptable, but it was a measure of changing times to see how hard it was for her to find an acceptable vocabulary to say so.

Character development improved. Some were still too bland, but some had edge and represented interesting dimensions of contemporary Ireland. Although characters (or their writers) almost never articulated any sort of ideological self-consciousness, they nevertheless embodied a number of ideological positions that played themselves out in both society and soap opera. Nicola Prendergast was an excellent embodiment of the yuppie mentality. She was never a caricature. She was well nuanced and kept nasty (against the tendency to soften long-running characters) and competitive. She was also vulnerable and human, but there was always a hard edge to her. Although she never said so, I imagined her to be someone who would vote PD and quote approvingly from opinion columns in the *Sunday Independent*. In contrast, other characters gave occasional expression to a social critique to the left: Charlie Kelly, Tara McCann, Malachy Costello and Barry O'Hanlon. This has never been developed very far, but there have been hints that some scriptwriters have something they might want to say through them.

Not surprisingly, the older characters represented traditionalist Ireland in a society not very respectful of its traditions. Mary O'Hanlon, now dead, was closer to the Irish mothers who populated *Tolka Row* and *The Riordans*. You could imagine her being able to talk to Rita Nolan or Mary Riordan and knowing where she was in the world. However, living in Dublin in the 1990s, she had no idea. Her son Barry had entered the seminary and she was set to be the mother of a priest, but he left and she had no idea how to communicate with him or with most of the other people she found around her. Paschal Mulvey was perhaps the strongest exponent of old values. He served with the Irish army in the Congo, but his identification with the military was far-reaching, as became apparent when he took to giving night classes in military history. Students who were living in the area went along for the laugh, but Paschal found it all quite unfunny. Eunice Phelan, like Mary, found it impossible to be the matriarch she wanted to be and failed to have any meaningful influence on her sons. Her mind was a dustbin of contradictory half-baked ideas, mixing old-fashioned Catholicism with tarot cards, horoscopes, reincarnation and celebrity gossip.

The women have been relatively liberated, in the sense that none of them is a full time housewife, living off a man's wages and a man's identity. Some are accomplished and ambitious. Others don't have glamourous careers, but they do a day's work, even if it is working behind the counter of a pub, sandwich bar or corner shop. There were lapses, such as Carol becoming a kept woman, whining about being bored watching *Oprah* all day and not even knowing that she had become a gangster's moll. There were other women living off their sexuality, Shelley doing so knowingly and shamelessly using it to get her way and set up a business and Tracey being seduced into prostitution through weakness and stupidity. At the other end of the scale, Annette was a solicitor who decided that she wanted a child. After almost seducing a young man for his sperm, she opted for an anonymous donor, only to discover it couldn't be done in Ireland without a partner and went to England for 'another Irish solution to an Irish problem'. Going against stereotypes in their jobs were Robin, a car mechanic, and Tess, a taxi-driver. The discourse about gender and the workplace was knowing, sometimes playfully, sometimes not. In discussing what sort of person their new boss might be, Niamh asked Paul if he would prefer a man or a woman. He replied: a man. She asked why. 'To keep the lad quota up', he said, 'Besides, with a man there are no mood swings or hidden agendas'. With Conor, however, the tone was not so lighthearted and a sexual harassment storyline ensued.

The kinds of relationships explored have been more various. Eoghan Healy was an important character in exploring alternative paths. He came into Carrigstown as a student (if I remember correctly, DCU was named as the university) working his way through college. He was on good terms with the females of his age and attractive to them. He talked through his coming out with them. Carrigstown took it in its stride and he subsequently became a teacher in the local school. He was conscientious in his work and in his relationships, but this did not exactly reap rewards. He developed a relationship with Liam, who was bisexual and married, and did not deal with him very honestly. Then he took up with Andrew, a fellow teacher, who had a partner dying of AIDS, who wanted help to die when the time came. Andrew would not do so, but Eoghan did. Simon's relatives denounced Eoghan in a crowded school hall. Not only was his career as a teacher in ruins, but he was questioned by the gardaí and the last we heard the case was being forwarded for prosecution. Moreover, Andrew was distant and unsupportive. Whatever became of Eoghan and this case? He has distant from Carrigstown, but could he not send an e-mail to another character to let us know? Storylines involving Eoghan, particularly about his coming out, received particularly high ratings. The progress of these stories was the subject of much comment in *Gay Community News*.[47]

The norms of sexual morality have shifted dramatically in both soap opera and society. There might be stray eyebrows raised about Eoghan, but the dominant point of view on how his character and situations were constructed was that he was a person of high moral character, whereas those who messed with him were not. More recently a lesbian character came on the scene. Camille, a high executive in Transglobal, entered into a marriage of convenience with Conor. Conor proposed to Nicola that they carry on their affair, despite the shock to her upon discovering his marriage. He proposed a relationship of 'no conventions, no restrictions'. Nicola's assertion that it was against her principles did not come across as stemming from the sixth commandment, but from yuppie respectability and property relations. Nicola's mother spoke not of sin, but of not bringing her up 'to be a loser' and advised her 'to get the business side of it under control'.

On abortion, there have been two stories. Niamh became pregnant by Leo and went to England to do what many Irish women have done, without much soul-searching. A more maturely explored and morally nuanced story came when Kay and Malachy, who treated the news of pregnancy with joy, found themselves on the horns of an agonising ethical and emotional dilemma after the amniocentesis. The child would be severely disabled. With great regret,

47 *Gay Community News*, Dublin 1996, cited by Lance Pettitt in *Screening Ireland* (Manchester: Manchester University Press, 2000), p. 183.

1 Éamon Kelly as Séamus in *Brigit* by Tom Murphy (1988).

2 Joe Lynch and Robert Carrickford as Dinny and Stephen in *Glenroe*.

3 Robert Carrickford, Emmet Bergin and Gerry Sullivan as Stephen, Dick and Mick in *Glenroe* (1988).

4 Mick Lally, Mary McEvoy, Donall Farmer, Maureen Toal and Robert
Carrickford as Biddy, Miley, Tim, Teasy and Stephen in *Glenroe*.

5 Eithne McGuinness as Gracie Tracey, Donall Farmer as Tim Devereux
and Mick Lally as Miley Byrne in the final episode of *Glenroe* (2001).

6 Michelle Holden as Blaithín Keaveney in *Nighthawks* (1990).

7 Máire Hastings as Sarah in *Ros na Rún* (1992).

8 Dearbhla Crotty and Alan Devlin as father and daughter in *Gold in the Streets* in the *Two Lives* series (1993).

9 Margot Jones and Robert O'Mahoney as Maria and William Kirwan in
The Mystery of Ireland's Eye in the *Thou Shalt Not Kill* series (1994).

10 Satraj Singh Suman and Laura Brennan as Shan Mohangi and Hazel Mullen in *The Green Tureen* in the *Thou Shalt Not Kill* series (1994).

11 Paidi Sayers (*centre*) in *The Kerry Killings* in the
Thou Shalt Not Kill series (1994).

12 Andrea Irvine and Seán McGinley as Detective Garda Moya O'Donnell
and Detective Sergeant Carl McCadden in *Making the Cut* (1997).

13 Andrew Connolly as Finn and Cathryn Harrison as
Catherine Kennedy in *Making the Cut* (1997).

14 Brenda Fricker in *Relative Strangers* (2000).

15a A scene from *A Love Divided* (2000).
15b Liam Cunningham (*centre*) in a scene from *A Love Divided* (2000).

16 Dermot Morgan as *Father Ted*.

Kay went to England and had an abortion. Malachy could not accept it. The edgy painful relationship between them after it was dealt with in a protracted and sophisticated way, although it did not seem to be popular with the audience.

For most of the time, the characters lived their lives outside the norms of Catholic sexual morality with very little in the way of moral discourse about it. The Irish state has legalised divorce, but the church has not changed its teaching, but it did not deter characters from divorcing and hoping to remarry (Paul and Nicola, for example). The adulterous affair between Dolores in an advanced stage of pregnancy and Frank in the house doing work on the new baby's nursery definitely pushed at the boundaries of transgression. So too was Billy's view that 'sex is a commodity to be sold like anything else'.

Fair City has tacitly tracked the secularisation of Irish society. It was assumed that most of the characters were Catholic, but that it impacted little on their lives. There was never a parish priest as a core character. It was part of the back story of Barry O'Hanlon when the serial began that he had intended to be a priest and he has consistently acted as a sort of secularised variant. As with many ex-priests or ex-seminarians, the impulse to be responsible for others, to articulate higher values, was still there, with or without a deity. He was first the manager of the community centre, then a teacher and finally headmaster of the local school. He resisted his mother's efforts to get him to teach at his old school, staffed by a religious order.

The first time a priest entered Carrigstown as a core character was when Malachy Costello appeared, as the nephew of Eunice Phelan, on leave from the foreign missions. He had come from the Philippines and went off again to Brazil. He was one of those priests who believed that they belonged with the poor and oppressed. He was regarded by his order as a bit of a loose cannon and inclined to cross the line in relating religion to politics. His discussions with his religious superior and with various characters from time to time in McCoy's pub have been among the more reflective bits of dialogue to occur in the series. He has been one of the most interesting characters that *Fair City* has developed. He became involved in a relationship with Kay McCoy and eventually became laicised and married. It was not happily ever after. He could not settle into private domesticity or confine his role in the community to being a publican. He still felt a sense of vocation and a pull to those struggling from below. The laicisation story was done far more credibly than in *Glenroe*. His subsequent preoccupation with greyhounds and gambling seemed more like recycled *Glenroe* cliché than meaningful exploration of character.

The representation of criminality in *Fair City* has been in contrast to other dramatisations of crime and criminals of this period. There were no less than three full-scale dramatic productions of the life of the notorious Dublin criminal boss, Martin Cahill, who was shot dead in 1994. John Boorman's feature film *The General* and BBC-Northern Ireland's *Vicious Circle* gave a romanticised portrayal of Cahill as a pidgeon-fancying Robin Hood. Brendan Gleeson, who played Cahill in Boorman's film, also played a romanticised criminal in *I Went Down*. This has been a persistent tendency in Irish film and television (as argued in my earlier book) of liberal indulgence of lumpen life and a tendency to make criminality chic and cute. It also manifested itself in other 1990s Irish productions, such as *Making Ends Meet* and *Ordinary Decent Criminal*.

In *Making the Cut* and *Fair City* RTÉ departed from this and gave a darker portrayal. The characterisation of Billy Meehan was better grounded and more plausible. He was working-class in origin, nice looking and could turn on a certain kind of charm when he wanted. He played mind games on those he drew into his web and could change from the hail-fellow-well-met persona to an insidious intimidator in a flash. The pull of his psychological seductions and the ruthlessness of his purposes were clearly shown. There was a certain implicit sympathy for those he drew into criminality, Leo, Lorcan, Carol, Tracey, but they were not indulged as blameless. Billy was not indulged at all in the text. The storylines involving drugs, prostitution, murder were played out in overt reference to real events in the current affairs of the time. At one point Leo said: 'Look what happened to Veronica Guerin' and a detective delivered a put-down to Billy as 'You're not the general, Billy.'

There was also a knowing reference to past and present media representations of law and crime. Pauline pleaded with Leo: 'This isn't *High Noon*, you know' and Billy in cajoling-menacing mode put it to Leo: 'It's not exactly *The Sopranos*, is it?' This was not Dublin in 'the rare old times'. It was not the fair city of fishmongers, of cockles and mussels, alive-alive-o. No, this was a Dublin of hotmail and health clubs, of sex in the city, of clubbing and cocaine, of refugees and racism, of crime and compassion, of poverty and property, of books and websites and universities. They were ready for the millennium bug and the euro changeover. These were the descendants of Molly Malone. Little Oisin went to yoga classes. Charlie, whose ancestor was a cooper in Guinness in 1832, drank his pints and observed that the *Little Book of Calm* should be the *Little Book of Profit*. It's all marketing these days, he thought. Unlike any previous RTÉ serials, *Fair City* had a website.[48]

What sort of picture of contemporary Ireland has emerged from *Fair City*?, I asked various people involved in the production of it. It's the *Evening Herald*, said Kevin McHugh, its script editor from 1995. It is dealing with the problems of ordinary people along the social spectrum ranging from the

---

48 There is a *Fair City* website at www.rte.ie/tv/faircity/.

criminal to the yuppie. Asked about restrictions, he replied that the only pressure was the pre-watershed slot. This had not kept it from dealing with AIDS, abortion, homosexuality. There was sometimes negative audience reaction, such as the scene when two gay men were about to kiss and another when Dr Jack made a remark about nurses and bedpans (which brought outraged calls from nurses). However, he believed that 'You can tell any story, if you tell it fully, properly, organically.'[49]

John Lynch, who was exective producer in the mid-90s, said that it was a view of working class people becoming less downtrodden and more aware of the world around them.[50] Niall Mathews, who was executive producer in 1991–2 and again since 1998, emphasised how much it had evolved. 'It was like turning a tank around'. In the beginning, there was an assumption that an urban serial meant lots of rows, so there were rows and rows, but they were based on nothing. There was no depth. Over the years, they built a pool of writers, added credibility to storylines, improved production values, increased the audience. About how it represented contemporary Ireland, he answered that he didn't directly set out to do that. In response to my argument about the potentiality of the soap opera in relation to the social order, he welcomed me to pitch any storyline that would enhance it.[51]

To the same question, Cathal Goan, then director of television and now director-general, commented, 'It's about 70% there.'[52] Bob Collins, Director-General, looked at its evolution and argued that it had eventually claimed its space and reflected urban life at work and at home. It had tackled difficult issues, such as abortion, which had brought criticism, but it was the degree of acceptance that was more striking.[53]

49 Interview with Kevin McHugh, 29 August 2001.   50 Interview with John Lynch, 18 August 2001.
51 Interview with Niall Mathews, 31 July 2001.   52 Interview with Cathal Goan, 29 August 2001.
53 Interview with Bob Collins, 11 September 2001.

CHAPTER 3

TnaG/TG4 drama

Ros na Rún

There was another new soap opera on the scene during this time. It was rural, but took a more robust approach to rural life than *Glenroe*. *Ros na Rún* (The headland of the secrets) was set in Dublin and in the Connemara gaeltacht in the west of Ireland. It was made in the Irish language with English subtitles. It began in 1992 with six episodes on RTÉ. The initial story began with Seán, a Dublin yuppie, taking up a job as manager of a chocolate factory in Connemara. He had never taken seriously the Irish he learned at school and tended to use it only when abroad. He was delighted to find Caitríona, an old college friend, working in the local radio station there, not realising at first that she was involved with Micheál, the foreman at the factory, who believed he should have got his job. Caitríona was determined to set up a no-holds-barred comment line. Seán seemed to walk into trouble wherever he went. A thorn in his side was Liam, the son in the b&b where he was residing. Liam was into heavy metal and motorbikes and stole Seán's keys and stayed in his Dublin flat. The old language cassette Seán was using to bring his rusty Irish up to scratch was woefully inadequate to talk of Metallica and Nintendo in the 90s gaeltacht. The ratings were high and the critics, including myself, welcomed it, thought it showed promise, although it remained to be seen 'whether or not this new soap can really work up a proper lather'[1] as one critic put it.

The suds drained away, as it turned out, as Udarás na Gaeltachta withdrew funding and Teílifís na Gaeilge took longer than anticipated to come on air. There were also differences of opinion as to its method of production. Cathal Goan, the ceannasai (chief executive) of TnaG at the time, wanted to build a permanent set, whereas Con Bushe, the original producer, wanted it less locked into sets and more using single camera on real locations.[2] The set was

---

[1] Eddie Holt, *Irish Independent*, 29 December 1992. I reviewed it on RTÉ Radio (*The Arts Show*) in December 1992. [2] Interviews with Cathal Goan (29 August 2001) and Con Bushe (12 September 2001).

built in Connemara. The serial then began again in 1996 when it became a flagship production of the new TnaG (now TG4). In 2001 it was going out twice a week with an omnibus edition as well.

The return of 'the not so sleepy village in the wild west of Ireland' bore a resemblance to the old image of the gaeltacht as a place of báinín jumpers and tin whistles and céilís, but it was also a land of e-mail and mobile phones and multimedia installations and the morning-after pill. When the morning-after pill didn't work, it was somewhere where a student called an abortion clinic, saying there were numbers all over UCG,[3] and took a plane from Galway to London. Nevertheless, if Ciara believed it was her right to choose, Nancy thought it was murder and said so. It was a place where two men could have a long-term homosexual relationship and raise a child, but was still a place where someone remembered that it was once a mortal sin. *Ros na Rún* too has shown the secularisation of Irish society. Religion seemed to play little role in it, but it was still there. There was not a priest among the core characters, but sometimes an extra came in as a priest to bless the new lifeboat or something like that. There were obvious differences in attitude to religion between characters. When Bernie's mother spoke of prayer, she replied: 'Things are complicated enough without bringing God into it.'

The contrast between the old and the new manifested itself in all sorts of ways. Sometimes it was very deliberate and self-conscious, using a student project on how life had changed in *Ros na Rún*. Other times it was casual. When older characters used quaint turns of phrase and expressed quaint notions, the young ones just rolled their eyes and proceeded to say and do things in their own way. Sometimes they took them on. Labhras (some called him Chicken Larry), the windbag manager of the radio station, complained that the youth were neglecting the genitive case. Liam thought that he was a grammar fascist, but rather than confront him, the younger staff set him up for a fall. The co-workers in the radio station discussed who would be shop steward, or mother of chapel said one, it being the NUJ. They dealt lightly with those in power, whether far or near, sometimes through confrontation, but more often through irony and cunning.

It was described as a place of 'scandals, secrets, schemes, surprises'.[4] Even scandals from former times, still secrets, hatched schemes and threatened surprises. Máire, wanting to honour her ancestor who fought in the war of independence, persuaded her son Liam to do a radio programme on him and proposed a memorial. She went on about 'how people suffered in those days' and 'those who went out and fought for freedom' and how young people

---

3 University College, Galway, now NUI Galway. 4 There is a *Ros na Rún* website at www.tg4.ie/gaeilge/rosnarun/ or www.tg4.ie/english/rosnarun/.

should know. Catríona, having a go at Sinéad, whom she was accusing of running an abortion referral service, remarked that there might be no young people in times to come. Meanwhile, Coilin felt provoked to reveal that her ancestor was an informer. Coilin was often the voice of the past. When he was young, children were encouraged to write for the folklore society. The *maistear* had rejected his writings as too political. He found out how bitter the truth could be. His brother revealed to him that it was their father who shot another person in the village. He showed Síle his own version of the true story of Ros na Rún and she told him it was better than *Angela's Ashes*.

All sorts of plot lines have been and will be pursued. There has always been a greater freedom in Irish language programmes than English ones. There is an atmosphere of freedom surrounding TG4 drama. Interviewing Eilís ní Dhuibhne, who was writing for both *Glenroe* and *Ros na Rún*, it was striking to note the difference in discussing the process of one *vis-à-vis* the other. On *Ros na Rún*, she said, it was possible to do anything.[5]

Other drama

Another TnaG drama to find an admiring audience was *C U Burn*, a nine-part sitcom series in 1996 set in Donegal about two brothers, who were the local undertakers, who set up the world's first turf-burning crematorium. Written, produced and directed by Niall Mac Eamharcaigh, it took a surreal and irreverent stance. Their ambition to expand and modernise led them to run foul of their customers and the authorities with plots featuring funerals using dangerously over-laden currachs, a politician dying during sex, drug-smuggling in coffins and the confusion ensuing when two corpses were mixed up and returned to the wrong families. Its black humour made few concessions to political correctness.

Other TnaG/TG4 drama has been sparse, but there have been several: *Gleann Ceo*, a series set in a Donegal village whose garda station faced closure; *Muintir na Darach* (People of the Oak), a series tracing the adventures of three friends trying to raise money for an adventure holiday who stumbled upon the story of three monks entrapped during a Viking raid a thousand years before; *Kaislean Klaus* about a German who bought his dream house in Connemara. Others were single plays, such as *Draíocht* (Magic), written by and starring Gabriel Byrne, about tensions between parents from the point of view of an 11-year-old boy, as the army father was about to go off to the Congo in 1960s, and *Lipservice* by Paul Mercier, about a *múinteoir* and students in a Dublin secondary school during oral Irish exams.

5 Interview with Eilis ní Dhuibhne, 25 August 2001.

Scéalta o Theach na Mbocht or *Tales from the Poorhouse* was a co-production made by Crescendo Concepts for TnaG and RTÉ. It was written by Eugene McCabe and produced by Louis Lentin in 1998. It was premised on the belief that: 'We cannot truly know the past. We can only imagine it.' This was the product of truthful imagination. It was not expensive, but it was substantial and memorable. There was basically only one voice and one set in each. The interlocking stories were set in a workhouse in south Ulster in 1848. Each told the story of the famine as it impacted on one area from a different point of view. The four half-hour dramas were: *The Orphan, The Master, The Landlord, The Mother.*

CHAPTER 4

RTÉ, independent productions and co-productions

As the years went on, less and less drama was being produced in-house and more and more of it was being co-produced or commissioned. The escalating costs of drama production made co-production more imperative. Also legislation required RTÉ to commission independent production: RTÉ was to invest a certain percentage of its production budget (up to 20% by 1999) in independent production. The Independent Productions Unit (IPU) was set up in 1994 and commissioned a number of programmes in a number of genres, including drama. Even co-productions came to be outsourced to independent production companies. The independent sector was building up in Ireland in the 1980s and grew even more rapidly in the 1990s. The growth of this sector was also supported by various schemes supported by the European Union and the Irish Film Board.

Some commissions had literary sources. Maeve Binchy's novel *Echoes* was made by Working Title for RTÉ and Channel 4 in four parts in 1988. It was set in the 1950s in County Waterford. It was soft, but vividly evocative of the times. There were the archetypal authoritarian nuns shaping the consciousness of all those quivering young women. Gone forever now are all those Sister Immaculatas and how they might ask of you: 'What hope is there for any girl who can't keep fresh water in the vase for Our Lady's flowers?' As to the plot, the *Irish Independent* critic called it 'Enid Blyton meets *The Thorn Birds*'. It twittered along harmoniously, he thought, 'then turned into a cacophony of suicidal screams and adulterous grunts'.[1] Other Maeve Binchy novels seen on television during these years were *The Lilac Bus* and *Circle of Friends*.

Then there was a Gandon Productions re-make of *The Real Charlotte* by Somerville and Ross. It was the company of Niall McCarthy, who had been RTÉ head of drama in the 1980s. It was expensive and it looked well, but why? There was so little drama in production at the time, so why re-make what was

---

1 Eddie Holt, *Irish Independent*, 30 April and 21 May 1998.

made before? There were also the *Dick Francis Mysteries* co-produced by RTÉ and Comedia in 1990.

Television over the decades relied less and less on theatrical sources, but there were still instances of it. *Beckett on Film* was a big project undertaken by Blue Angel and Tyrone Productions for RTÉ and Channel 4 with the Irish Film Board.[2] It employed a panoply of leading international directors to film all nineteen plays of Samuel Beckett. RTÉ and Channel 4 transmitted them in a televisual extravaganza in March 2001. They were also given cinematic screening at the Irish Film Centre in February 2001, occasioning discussion of the relationship between theatre and film. However, most who saw them saw them on television. Probably many taped them, because they were worthy and should be archived, but never got around to watching them. The use of close-up and concentration on the subtleties of facial expression was an obvious way that both film and television could do something distinctive in giving new production to these plays.

Directors let loose and tried all sorts of innovative ways of bringing the distinctiveness of another medium to the texts. Neil Jordan, for example, in *Not I* reduced the whole visual dimension to the mouth to give a sense of the disembodied voice. The transition to television was bound to be much more radical than cinema, because the stark abstraction, the decontextualised time and space, and the existentialist futility, must have seemed very strange within the flow of the television schedule. I would like to have experimented with that but I was in Cape Town giving e-mail instructions about taping the series; I saw them, as did many others on tape. They did not top the TAMs, but were undertaken by RTÉ in its interpretation of its responsibilities as a public service broadcaster. There were some curmudgeonly letters to editors scoffing at the project and wondering if anybody was actually watching them, but the project was generally appreciated. As to substantive analysis of the plays, there are other sources for that. The secondary literature on Beckett is enormous, and a book on television drama is unlikely to add much to it. Personally I found Beckett's plays most evocative when going through my existentialist phase, but after moving on, not in the direction of postmodernism, less so. Beckett's work does match the postmodernist mentality and so still has much contemporary resonance.

There was a steady stream of short dramas under the *Short Cuts* scheme co-funded by the Irish Film Board/Bord Scannan na hÉireann (IFB/BSÉ) and transmitted by RTÉ. They were designed particularly to encourage new talent and to emphasise visual flair and a fresh look at contemporary Ireland. Occasionally they were made by more experienced writers and directors.

2 For more information on this project, see www.beckettonfilm.com.

Before I Sleep was written and directed by Paul Mercier and was a day in the life of an unemployed Dubliner on an odyssey through the city. *The Breakfast*, written and directed by Peter Sheridan, was about a boy delivering breakfast to a Christian Brother, finding him dead and eating the breakfast. Some themes dealt with in others were: bullying, orgasm, homosexuality, hunger strikes, debt, crime, international romances, greyhounds, ballroom dancing.

There was also the *First View* and then the *Debut* slot for up-and-coming directors. Some themes of these were: a gay youth imagining coming out, a father disappointed at a son not into football, dying of AIDS. *Straight to Video*, made by Hill 16 and shot on digital video, was a comic series of faux video diaries.

There were a number of feature films funded by RTÉ or IFB/BSÉ or both, which received cinematic distribution as well as television transmission.[3] Some of these were:

Korea	*November Afternoon*
Guiltrip	*Ordinary Decent Criminal*
Ailsa	*Trojan Eddie*
Snakes and Ladders	*Sweety Barrett*
Last of the High Kings	*Boys and Men*
The Sun	*The Boy from Mercury*
The Moon and the Stars	*I Went Down*
The Disappearance of Finbarr	*Nora*
Saltwater	

A number of these were seen primarily and reviewed as films, whereas others were primarily seen on television. The themes were various: suffocating relationships in an army town (*Guiltrip*); brother-sister incest (*November Afternoon*); criminals on the romp (*I Went Down*).

The *Real Time* slot on RTÉ featured: *Just in Time*, a Sampson Films production about two couples over an awkward candlelit dinner full of evasions, repetitions, silences; *Making Ends Meet*, an Indi Films crime caper about a kid in trouble in school who idolised his father who had to hurry his robberies to sign on the dole; and *Double Carpet*, a Pegasus Productions story about horses, gambling, relationships and gambling on relationships. *JJ Biker* was about a haemophiliac dying of AIDS who wanted to drive a motorbike before he died.

Some international co-productions were set in several countries and dealt with migration patterns and even the cosmopolitan character of contemporary life as well as the things that slip through its cracks. *Sara*, co-produced by

3 For more information on these films, see www.iol.ie/filmboard/ or www.rte.ie/tv/ipu.

RTÉ, France 3 and Edinburgh Film and Video Production in 1995, was a French-English bilingual six-part series set in the Camargue in which Sara, brought up since infancy by gypsies, was reunited with her Irish family. *Flesh and Blood* in 1998 was another Irish-French co-production set in Ireland and France about two estranged brothers.

Relative Strangers in 2000 was a four-part serial developed by the IPU in RTÉ, produced by Little Bird with Tatfilm of Düsseldorf. It opened showing the lives of an Irish family living in Germany. Maureen Lessing was celebrating her fiftieth birthday, obviously highly regarded by her co-workers in a British forces psychiatric unit and living a comfortable domestic life with her husband, son and daughter in Düsseldorf. Her husband's sudden death – a heart attack when driving on a motorway – changed everything. Sorting out his affairs, all sorts of things came to light that did not make sense at first. Eventually, following the trail back to Ireland, she discovered that he had another family. Liza Becker, she discovered, was an Austrian woman living in Bray with a son. Strangers to each other, they confronted the traumas of bereavement, deception and impoverishment. Adding to the drama was fatal disease, with the twist that the child of the one woman was suffering from leukaemia and the only hope for his life was a possible bone marrow donation by one of the children of the other. The landscape of contemporary life, the characterisation, the production were all credibly stitched together. It was well received. It also resulted in a large number of calls from people wanting information on how to become bone marrow donors.

CO-PRODUCTION AND 'TROUBLES' DRAMA

Over the years there were a number of British-Irish co-productions giving a dramatic treatment to the troubles past and present. *The Treaty* was an RTÉ-Thames drama documentary in 1991 marking the seventieth anniversary of the Anglo-Irish treaty of 1921. It was meticulous and credible in its reconstruction of the negotiations. *Events at Drimaghleen* was a BBC Northern Ireland and RTÉ drama-documentary piecing together tragic events of 1988, made in 1991. *Force of Duty*, a BBCNI and RTÉ psychological-political drama in 1992, conveyed the breakdown and subsequent suicide of an RUC detective under pressure following the killing of his colleague.

Rebel Heart, a Picture Palace production for BBCNI, RTÉ, IFB/BSÉ and Irish Screen in 2000, was a four-part serial on the Irish rebellion written by Ronan Bennett. The historical events from the Easter Rising in 1916, through the war of independence to the treaty in 1921 were focused on the life of one volunteer 'torn between love and the fight for freedom'. It was a 'Mills and

Boon' version of the Irish rebellion. The central relationship between Ernie Coyne and Ita Feeney, a rebellious lass shooting a gun and showing her thigh in Stephen's Green during Easter week, was love at first sight. It featured James Connolly saying, 'There's going to be a bloodbath' with the relish of a pre-adolescent boy playing Power Rangers. It gave crude and clichéd treatment to class, sex and nation. It was expensive and empty. It was embarrassing. It was a waste of resources. BBC, RTÉ, everybody involved, should have known better. It bombed in ratings and reviews, at least in Ireland. However, the BBC shop website selling the video quotes rave reviews from British sources:[4] 'Beautifully filmed with an exceptional cast and fine dialogue' (*Guardian*); 'As a piece of drama this is as good as television gets' (*Irish Post*, London).

Another co-production on the terrain of the troubles was *Act of Betrayal* from RTÉ along with ABC (Australia), Revcom (France) and Griffith Productions (UK). It concerned an IRA man on the run in Australia. It was a glossy lowest-common-denominator fantasy in which an IRA volunteer, sickened by the struggle, walked into an RUC station, turned himself into a supergrass, then got sent by the British government to Australia to live like *Neighbours*. There was one particularly ludicrous scene where this Irish male set out to seduce an Australian female who needed as much seducing as a politician needed persuading to show up to a photo-opportunity. His technique was to chat her up with an *Ireland for Beginners* account of the Famine. She was practically polishing her diaphragm, while he was still working his way up to 1847, observed Gene Kerrigan.[5]

Eureka Street, although it claimed that all stories were love stories, was more a Troubles farce. It was a four-part adaptation of the Robert McLiam Wilson novel made by Euphoria Films for BBCNI and RTÉ. It was, we were told, 'Belfast as you've never seen it before'. This was true enough. It subordinated orange and green to black comedy. Jake Jackson, from a Catholic background, practised his trade as a repo man with ecumenical equanimity. Chuckie Lurgan, his best friend, was an unemployed and overweight Prod obsessed with cars, money and fame, all of which he seemed to have no hope of ever having, until one day when he hatched a bold scheme: a giant dildo offer for £9.99, which brought in hundreds of cheques, which he cashed, and sent back refund cheques with 'giant dildo refund' stamped on them. Of course, no one would cash them. On the strength of having turned an initial investment of £22.47 into £42,743, he applied for a £1.2 million grant from the Ulster Development Board.

There was a hilarious scene where Chuckie went before this board and pulled off the most stunning bluff, full of pseudo-radical management jargon,

---

4 See www.bbc.co.uk.   **5** Gene Kerrigan, *Sunday Tribune*, 11 September 1998.

presenting a business plan 'so innovative, so radical', 'a golden opportunity', 'a new Ulster'. Until now, he explained, profit was king, but 'let me paint a different picture for you': production and distribution, not separate, all one, unit profit at point of sale, export opportunities, a multinational corporation centred in Belfast. All this with no mention whatsoever of any product or service. He got the money and bought a big flashy car, expensive clothes, drink for his friends. Basically he spent and consumed. He became a media star, got a girl and, before long, still producing nothing, an American was prepared to invest £20 million in Lurgan Enterprises.

The Troubles were there all the time and there to be sent up as well. In the pub, where Chuckie was celebrating his windfall with his friends, there was a poetry reading by a republican ex-prisoner. One poem (in Irish translated into English) was: '*From a sniper to a British soldier who is about to die*: You never saw me … for 800 years … stealing my wealth, tormenting my people …' Getting into an argument with the translator, Jake expressed his alienation from the various forces of national liberation, to which she said: 'We just want to express our culture,' to which he said: 'preferably with kalashnikovs.' The hard men on both sides were parodied in many ways. A threat on a door read: 'YOUR DED.' It was basically more of a peace process drama, however. It showed the embers of the Troubles smouldering, sometimes flaring, but the whole mood and the whole scam was built on the atmosphere of building anew from the rubble. One scene was a ceasefire party and another showed the announcement of news of the Good Friday Agreement. On a television current affairs programme, Chuckie, who never concerned himself much with politics, gave vague answers to specific questions and was hailed as a great new political visionary and was asked if he was going to form a new political party. With bewilderment and bluff, and some real conviction too, he argued that the problem of Northern Ireland was lack of jobs, that people were fed up with all the sectarian shite. Then he launched into Martin Luther King: 'I have a dream' mode … where the sons of the Ulster plantation and people who like *Riverdance* would live together. The final episode ended with a voice over from Jake: 'I don't know what got into Chuckie that year … but despite everything that had happened and would happen, anything seemed possible.' It caught the mood of 1999. It was well received and won awards.

Another somewhat lighthearted treatment of the Troubles made by BBCNI in association with RTÉ in 1994 was *Henri*, about a 10-year-old Protestant girl travelling to Belfast to play the accordion in a music festival, with a last minute change in accommodation arrangements resulting in her staying with a Catholic family. It also won awards. There were a number of other Troubles dramas made by BBCNI without RTÉ.

CO-PRODUCTION AND HISTORICAL DRAMA

Drama of famine and emigration

Other co-productions went further back into Irish history for their subject matter. *The Hanging Gale* was a four-part serial made by Little Bird for BBCNI and RTÉ in 1995. It was set in Donegal in 1846 during the Famine and featured the four McGann actor-brothers as the Phelan brothers struggling to save the land and lives of their family. It opened with Ribbonmen[6] assassinating the English land agent. The new land agent was a different sort, one who experienced moral dilemmas and sympathised with the people whose lives were ravaged by potato blight, harsh rents, violent evictions and wasting hunger. Nevertheless, his loyalty to the landlord triumphed over his qualms of conscience. Meanwhile, the brothers had their own choices to make: to fight for their homes or go to the poorhouse, to go on the run or to gaol, to pray for better times or engage in rebellion. It was a worthy production, but somehow it was too glossy and too full of derring-do to convey effectively the desperation and devastation of the dispossessed.

Somehow the simpler and less expensive productions such as *Tales from the Poorhouse* in 1998 and *The Poorhouse* in 1996 conveyed more movingly and memorably the impact of the famine on the poor. The latter, by Ocean Films for RTÉ, was set in sepia and told the tale of a girl who was raped and died in childbirth from the point of view of a poorhouse undertaker, who was consumed with guilt about what he might have done to help her, and who prepared her body meticulously for burial. The end of it, which re-imagined her and her baby in twentieth-century Ireland, while he looked on from the 1840s, was a bit odd and unnecessary, but it was an effective production.

Some co-productions took as their basis the stories of the poor of nineteenth-century Ireland who emigrated. *Random Passage* was an eight-part serial in 2001 tracing the journey of Mary Bundle, an orphan in a Waterford workhouse, based on books by Bernice Morgan – *Random Passage* and *Waiting for Time*. The finance of £12 million [€15m] came from 22 different sources, including RTÉ and IFB, 70% from Canadian sources, much of it from the government of Newfoundland, where much of the story was set. The lush scenery and music, showing life in 1805 Ireland, was cinematic cliché, as were scenes in an English workhouse, the transatlantic passage, arrival in St Johns and the servant-master-mistress relationship in an early bourgeois household. It was harshly reviewed on this account. For Shane Hegarty:

---

6 Ribbonmen: an early nineteenth-century rural secret society, nationalist and anti-Establishment in tenor, precursor of the Fenian movement.

Random Passage is quite possibly the worst thing RTÉ will show this year, a relentlessly awful costume drama that trades on the fact that, because there are several extras in old costumes, it has got a love affair and because the action takes place in two countries, then it must be a sweeping epic ... Every fifth-generation Irish emigrant's half-baked idea of Ireland is thrown into a big blender, and squeezed out the other end as a fine blancmange that the producers hope will be gobbled up by viewers in the international territories. You'll see evictions! You'll see potatoes! There's a workhouse! Large families! Boat journeys! British baddies – boo! Feisty colleens – hooray! Terrible, realist poverty! Terrible, realistic poverty that luckily leaves everybody with nice teeth![7]

The teeth were definitely way too perfect for the lives the characters were supposed to have led. I did think that the early part of it, especially where it was set in Ireland, was twee. However, I thought that other parts of it were stronger and truer. The impression of the winters in the wilds of Newfoundland and of the relentlessly difficult lives of those who were building a settlement from scratch was memorable. It had a clarity about the workings of an early market economy, of the gap between those who lived a life of exceedingly hard labour and those who manipulated and appropriated their labour. It also gave a non-clichéd version of the complicity of Catholicism with primitive capitalism.

Another emigration tale, which was also panned, was *King of Grass Castles*, an Australian-Irish co-production in 1998, a four-part serial based on a Molly Durack novel. It was the rags-to-riches saga by numbers: lush scenes of Galway Bay, peasant poverty, famine, eviction, passage, striking gold. It was not that there was nothing left to say about this, the origin myth of many Irish Australians. It was that it reduced it to the clichés. It added no new angles, no new insights. It had not only been done before, but it had been done better, so why do this one?

Land of Hope, for example, was a ten-part Australian serial made by JNP Films in 1988, following the fortunes of an Irish family from 1890 to 1972. It not only shadowed the political history of Australia during those years, but made a stab at grappling with the big ideas and global movements of those decades: capital versus labour, capitalism versus socialism; even communism and feminism were dramatised intelligently. Personal and ideological conflicts surrounding the rise of the labour movement, the impact of the October Revolution, the ban on the Communist Party, the protests against the Vietnam War, the challenge of the women's movement – all were vividly recounted.

7 Shane Hegarty, *Irish Times*, 12 May 2001.

Drama and twentieth-century history

The ability to sketch social change through the lives of particular characters, when done well, is the stuff of great drama. An Australian production by Roadshow, in which ABC, RTÉ and Channel 4 were co-producers, which did this particularly well was *Brides of Christ* in 1991. The six-part series traced the lives of two young women who entered the convent in 1962 and registered the impact of Vatican II on the life of nuns. It captured, as well, the whole atmosphere of questioning received ideas and values that swept the world in the 1960s in a sensitive and fresh way. Brenda Fricker was Sister Agnes, voice of the old order, who had a difficult time on her hands when even novices started talking back. A particularly moving scene was one where an old nun took off her habit, knowing that it was for the last time.

Amongst Women

A much acclaimed serial was the adaptation of the novel by John Mc Gahern, *Amongst Women*. This was a tale of patriarchal domination intricately and insightfully observed. It opened in 1947 on a family in rural Ireland reciting the rosary. The mother had died and the father and his five children moved through their mundane routines. As if the world of the Catholic Church and Irish rural society were not already claustrophobic enough in the 1950s, the Morans lived in an even more claustrophic milieu in which 'The family is the heart of everything. Without it, we're nothing.' 'Raising a family is the most important job a man can undertake.' Every *fiat* of this most severe father was justified as 'in the best interests of the family'. There were to be no other considerations. Michael Moran was a devout Catholic. He was a citizen of a local community. He was a man who fought for the state in the war of independence. However, church and town and nation were inevitable forces, like nature, but not to be trusted. The family, turned in on itself, under control, was seen as the secure haven from all the rest. All the children and his second wife each negotiated their identity and their lives *vis-à-vis* his power over them. It was honest and relentless and memorable. It was well written, well acted, well made in every way. It deservedly won many awards.

Falling for a Dancer

Falling for a Dancer was also a Parallel Films production for BBCNI in association with RTÉ and IFB in 1998. It was also a four-part serial which was an adaptation of a novel. It was also on the same territory in that it was set in Ireland in past decades in a patriarchal Catholic rural household in which the mother had died and a second wife was brought into a difficult domestic set-up. The script and novel, both written by Deirdre Purcell, were set in the 1930s in Cork. It began with a young woman who found herself pregnant with the child of a travelling actor, faced with the choice between a Magdalen laundry or an arranged marriage to a widower with four children in the wilds of the Beara peninsula. It was well made and gave a vivid sense of bourgeois Catholic life in Cork city, the horrors of the workhouse 'for shop girls and servants', the harsh realities of rural life in west Cork. The problem with it was the 'Mills and Boon' love-at-first-sight storyline. Arriving in torrential rain, Mossy Sheehan took one look at Elizabeth Sullivan, carrying the child of one man and married that day to another, and was devoted to her forever. Despite all rebuffs and obstacles, he won the hand of the fair not-maiden. The serial ended with a stereotypical happy-ever-after wedding.

A Love Divided

A Love Divided was also a Parallel Films production for RTÉ and BBC Scotland in association with the Irish Film Board in 1998. It was set in Fethard-on-Sea in Wexford in the 1950s and based on a true story. When Seán Cloney, a Catholic farmer, married Sheila, who was Protestant, she signed the *Ne temere* pledge that was standard at that time, whereby the Protestant partner to a mixed marriage promised that the children would be brought up as Catholics. It showed them living a happy life on their farm and in their village. On Sundays, everyone in the village would be on the main town square. Seán and his daughters would attend mass at the Catholic church and Sheila and her father and sister would attend the Protestant service.

The trouble began when it was time for the oldest child to start school. Sheila balked at being bullied, and the whole town, except for the publican who was a non-believer who had fought in the war of independence, advised her not to make trouble. Even her Protestant pastor said: 'we keep our heads down and our mouths shut.' The Catholic priest, who had been shown railing against the lack of religious freedom 'behind the iron curtain', took the child out of the Protestant school. Sheila fled with her children, first to Belfast and then to Scotland. Seán went with the parish priest to the bishop, who advised him to say prayers for the conversion of heretics and schismatics. The priest organised a boycott against all Protestants in the town, and life became nasty, even violent. It was in the national press. Eventually Seán found Sheila and returned with her and the children and stood up to the priest. They did not send their children to school and kept themselves to themselves. The Vatican and the government forced the priest to end the boycott. In 1998 the then bishop of the diocese, Brendan Comiskey, formally apologised for the role played by the church in 1957. The family survived, but their relationship to the community had changed forever. Indeed, the community itself changed forever. It was an extreme episode, but the picture it drew of Catholicism in the 1950s was absolutely accurate. For those who did not live through it, this drama was there to show them.

CO-PRODUCTION AND CONTEMPORARY DRAMA

Family

Perhaps the darkest family drama of all was *Family*. This four-part series by Roddy Doyle, written for television, was a BBC-RTÉ co-production in 1994 set in 1990s Dublin. Each episode moved the story on in time, but each foregrounded a different member of the Spencer family.

Episode 1, *Charlo*, showed us the world of the father. Charlo Spencer was shown at home with his wife and four children and out and about socialising and engaging in criminal activity. He was seen eating, drinking, robbing, having sex with two different women, masturbating, partying, brutalising everything and everyone he touched. From him emitted a constant and casual cruelty. He radiated menace. The home was a battleground. Even when being momentarily jolly, a sense of fear registered on his children's faces, knowing that seeming benevolence could transmute into malevolence in an instant. Dublin looked dark and life seemed stark in this world of unemployment, petty crime and pointlessness.

Episode 2, *John Paul*, looked at this world through the life of the older son. At 13, John Paul Spencer was a Charlo in the making. While fearing his father, he wanted his attention and approval. He was full of bravado and bluff. In school he was class clown and troublemaker. He was already squaring up, not only to teachers, but to the gardaí, when they came to the house looking for stolen goods. With his peers, he bragged about running away from home, watching porn videos and 'getting his hole'. However, in other scenes, we saw the vulnerability he tried so hard to hide. When his parents fought, he would reach for his inhaler. At one point, he was so stressed that he wet himself and cried. Later, out in the dark, with bonfire burning and friends horsing around, he collapsed in a fit.

Episode 3, *Nicola*, took up the story of the oldest daughter from her first day at work as a machinist in a large clothing factory. The other women in the factory and on the bus, discussed sex in a bawdy way and fantasised about doing it with film stars. With her boyfriend, who was unemployed, there was tension from her having and his not having money, and from Charlo squaring up against him and leering at her. She was trying to find herself and make her way, but without a very firm basis. She was only semi-articulate. Her answer to most questions was: 'It was all right,' unless it was her little sister, often asking precocious questions about sex, to which she usually replied, 'Shut up'. There was constant tension and fighting in the house with a bit of temporary respite now and again as they watched *Fair City* on television. Through this episode, there were lascivious looks and hints of incest. Even the hint of it was the last straw for Paula, who turned the tables and assaulted Charlo. She literally kicked him out and packed all his possessions and put them out in the rain. From then on, life changed in the Spencer household. It didn't exactly become a haven of peace and light, but the tension began to ease. At first, Paula's extended family occupied the house to protect them in case Charlo returned. There were aunts, uncles, cousins everywhere and huge amounts of food were ordered. Eventually they all went home and a new normality began to establish itself.

Episode 4, *Paula*, concerned the life of the mother. Intercut with opening credits and aerial views of the city was Paula Spencer singing karaoke, singing a love song, the words utterly discordant with the reality of her life. In the supermarket, she didn't have enough money for groceries. Visiting her sisters, they told her that it had been two months and they were sick of her whingeing. Then, lightening up, they all agreed that she needed 'a good ride'. Even more, she needed a job and she got one and then two, 'twice as many as he ever had'. One was night cleaning in a city centre office and the other was one day a week cleaning a house in Howth for a professional couple. The second did not last as she stood up to the condescending manner of the woman giving her orders and told her to clean her own house. Just after, she confronted the principal of the school over John Paul's tattoo.

Coming and going and doing her night cleaning job, the sound track played 'Any day now, I shall be released.' And then 'I will survive'. When Charlo arrived at the door, three days late with something for John Paul's birthday and tried to talk his way back in, she struggled against weakening. When ingratiation didn't work, he mocked her for being a scrubber. As it ended, she sat at the dinner table with her four children and asked John Paul to say grace. 'It's stupid,' he said. Then he said he didn't know it. She insisted and he stumbled through. All said 'Amen' and ate. It wasn't so much a turning to religion. Indeed the absence of religion is a striking feature of Roddy Doyle's novels and plays. It was a reaching for order, even if it was off the shelf. It was like the words of karaoke songs. It was saying that they would survive. Life would still be difficult, but it had got better and maybe it would even get better again. Roddy Doyle took the story from there in a novel called *The Woman Who Walked into Doors* as he imagined her getting herself together to the point where she would sit at the kitchen table and begin to write her story to bring understanding and order to it.

Family stirred people up more than any television drama had done in a long time. There were calls to the Childline and Women's Aid helplines from those who recognised their truth in this fiction. Others came forward and told their stories on the media. The audience soared to 1.2 million. The critics praised it enthusiastically. Brendan Glacken in the *Irish Times* observed that it came days after the *Eurovision Song Contest*, which gave such an attractive picture of Ireland, one night after the re-screening of Doyle's *The Snapper*, which gave upbeat comic treatment of urban working class life and after years of *Glenroe* and *Fair City*, which went for soft treatment of difficult social issues. It was as if *Bambi* had been screened regularly for ten years to be suddenly replaced by *The Godfather.* He thought that RTÉ drama (although it was basically a BBC production) had come of age or at least it occupied heights unoccupied for twenty-five years.[8]

It was not all praise and plain sailing, however. Far from it. There were denunciations from politicians, priests, teachers and community groups, and calls upon the author to respond. Priests gave sermons against it for undermining the sanctity of marriage. Doyle admitted that this was exactly what he was doing. As for teachers, his own union condemned the portrayal of a teacher hitting a student. Doyle said that this was to swallow the lie that no teacher ever hit a student.[9] When it came to the community groups and the politicians coming in behind them, this was the most protracted controversy. The series was shot primarily in the Ballymun area of Dublin. Although it was never referred to as Ballymun in the script, the tower blocks of Ballymun were recognisable and didn't look like anywhere else in Ireland. However, the fictional place was on the DART line, which the real Ballymun wasn't. Doyle and the BBC saw it as a sort of universal landscape. However, the residents of Ballymun, particularly the community activists, saw it as Ballymun and judged the drama by documentary standards. They argued that their community was being stereotyped and held up to ridicule. They contended that it was a gross misrepresentation of working class life in the area and that such depiction did them harm:

> Ballymun is a community facing many disadvantages; it suffers an unemployment rate of 2.5 times the national average. The overwhelming majority of people in the area want to work, they want a decent future for their children. Ballymun is a vibrant community with over 90 groups active in the area. However, every time a programme such as *Family* is aired, it undermines the image of our community in the eyes of prospective employers, possible investors and the public at large.[10]

---

8 Brendan Glacken, *Irish Times*, 7 May 1994. **9** Roddy Doyle, 1999 interview on the internet magazine *Salon*, www.salon.com/books/feature/1999/10/28/doyle/index2.html. **10** Seán Kelly, Ballymun Job Centre, letter in the *Irish Times*, 12 May 1994.

Much has changed in Ballymun. With improving economic times, both investment and employment have risen. The Ballymun Regeneration Project has been a bold and democratic exercise in town planning and the towers are due for demolition. *Family* will stand as a realistic dramatisation of what life was like for many who lived in a certain time and a certain place. It was never meant to imply that everyone in Ballymun had such problems or that no one outside of Ballymun had such problems. I live in the Ballymun area myself and come across community activists more than criminals, but I would defend the veracity and validity of the series and believe that much of the controversy was talking at cross purposes and mangled in a mixing of registers.

Scene

Scene was a series of RTÉ co-productions with BBC (schools division) in 1996. *Edward No Hands* by Dermot Bolger was about a 15-year-old boy who hanged himself. It showed him growing up under pressure of macho attitudes from his father, telling him when he could barely ride a bike to do it with no hands. He was the target of bullies at school and made attempts to be a bully himself. He made up stories about himself and his father, and about himself and a girl, to impress the bullies (and himself). When the girl confronted him with his lies, he committed suicide. As he jumped from a tree with a rope around his neck, he said, 'Look, da, no hands.' RTÉ postponed transmission, as it was scheduled to go out during a week of media debate about the suicide of Dublin poet and AIDS activist Pat Tierney.

Radio Waves by Bernard Farrell was about a young woman, who had been to university, coming back to her home town to look after her widowed mother and take up a job in the local radio station. She set about organising issue-oriented programmes about women's health, widows' pensions, traveller accommodation and unemployment. She shook things up and met with opposition. Her mother, who believed that 'a woman on her own is an embarrassment', was mortified at her 'giving cheek to councillors'. The station manager was ever more displeased, and she lost her job. As she left town, however, there were indications that she had made her mark on her mother, friend and co-worker.

Career Opportunities by Declan Hughes was about a young woman in a big office who got fired when she resisted sexual advances from her boss, and about different attitudes to sexual harassment. These were modest but focused and competent plays, made to stimulate discussion in a school environment but also to cause reflection in a more general audience.

Paths to Freedom

Paths to Freedom was a six-part series by Grand Pictures for RTÉ in 2000, done in faux documentary style, tracking the trials and tribulations of two ex-prisoners. The fly-on-the-wall camera crews followed the two from the time of their release. Jeremy, a consultant gynaecologist from south County Dublin, spent a year in Mountjoy for a drunk-driving episode that resulted in paralysis for an asylum seeker. Rats, an unemployed poet and musician, from inner city Dublin, was a frequent offender.

Their lives offered themselves to constant contrast in terms of class. Jeremy's difficulties related to getting his book *Women Inside Out* published, an interview about it with Gerry Ryan not going as planned, facing a committee judging his fitness to practice and investigating the refugee he paralysed. His wife sided with him, saying that the refugee probably engineered the accident. Rats found it hard to hold down a job, first having a go at security, then smiley burgers. His wife left him and went off to Belfast with his kids and her lover. He refused to continue the documentary unless the crew helped him make a video for his new band 'Sperm.com'. At one point, they both returned to Mountjoy to address inmates on the effects of prison and release. Jeremy's considered response: 'Before this unmitigated fiasco, I had a handicap of 9, now it's 15 *and* I've lost my no claims bonus.' Rats, on the other hand, had some fond memories of prison, particularly the opportunity to take courses such as 'repressed spiritualism and the struggle of the inner child in the work-place'. Over six episodes, it was unevenly amusing, but it definitely had its moments.

Black Day at Black Rock

Black Day at Black Rock in 2001 took head-on the issue of refugees, increasingly prominent in the public discourse during this time. It came out of an actual incident, which aggravated writer and director Gerard Stembridge so much that he sought an RTÉ commission to do something about it, which he achieved without hesitation. It was set in a small Irish town where thirty refugees were about to arrive. In various sites in the town, the shop, the school, the hairdressers, the hotel, the school, the streets, the homes, all were having their say.

Almost every possible position was taken by somebody. Certainly every possible racist cliché was trotted out. These people, 'busloads of ballubas', would bring disease, AIDS and whatever. They, 'the sweepings of whatever country dumped them on us', were criminals and chancers, who couldn't speak the language, but knew every sort of scam. They would be lounging around in luxury, sponging on the taxpayers. They would go to the local school, and young black bucks would be going for the town's daughters and 'Sex for these lads wouldn't be the holy sacrament it is for us.' Who was going to protect poor pensioners from being assaulted by them in their beds? What about their own poor? Before they knew it, the town would be overrun by these people. Why so many? Why their town? There was no democratic consultation. It was tyranny, taking advantage of a small town that didn't have its own TD. Meanwhile, they bought Aunt Jemima pancakes and Uncle Ben's rice. They loved nachos and Italian breadsticks. They put their pennies in the mission box in the shop. The school was named for St Martin de Porres. They did like Denzel Washington films. The travel agency specialised in exotic locations. The doctor and the gombeen's wife booked their tryst in Bali, where, they were assured, the locals were really friendly.

On the other side was a '60s radical who grew organic food, huffing and puffing in righteousness and in full rhetorical flight against all the arguments of the rest. In the school, when the youth were asked, they thought that it would be something different, 'a bit of *craic*'. In the hotel, where the refugees would stay, the owner asserted that it was a chance to do the right thing, to broaden the horizons of the young people. Of course, she would be paid £25 per person per night. £25 x 30 x 7 x 52, the locals calculated with envy and rage. The teacher, preparing to chair the town meeting, spoke to the civil servants in charge of the placement. He spoke of doing the right thing and broadening horizons and they spoke of complying with EU directives. He explained his teaching methods, of using everyday texts to illuminate historical situations, and they asked if it helped with exams. He asked if they might tell some of the stories of the refugees, as it might help locals to connect with them. No, that would not do, they said, the stories had not been verified and the statistic was that 70% were not telling the truth.

At the town meeting that night, all of these argumentative strategies were repeated with a few more added to put a more sophisticated face on it. Over the years, a 'delicate balance' had been struck between natives and friendly foreigners, but thirty in one fell swoop would disrupt this delicate balance. Another spoke of his passionate desire to do the right thing, not only for themselves, but for these poor people. The town didn't have the facilities. It would be too much of a burden on the doctor. They needed to take care of their own poor and homeless. The town simpleton asked, as he was primed, could he live in Ard na Rí as well and have £15 pocket money? That would be a matter for the Department of Social Welfare or the local health board, not the Department of Justice, the civil servants replied.

The organic radical got up to cast scorn, but no one wanted to hear. Then her son rose and asked simply why were people afraid? To him, it all sounded interesting and exciting. Why shouldn't everybody mix together and why shouldn't that become normal? The teacher then read a letter from a famine emigrant who wrote home after arriving in America about how difficult it all was, all mixing together, not knowing whom you could trust, including your own, missing home, but still seeing that it was an adventure, a chance. Later that night the hotel burned down. A homeless man of the town not only died in the fire, but was set up to look as if he had started it. The Celtic Coaches bus arrived full of black people, all clean and chatty and ready for whatever life might offer. The firemen declared the hotel uninhabitable, and the bus turned back, and the locals who got their way laughed. Meanwhile the doctor and the gombeen wife went off saying, 'We can go anywhere', while the soundtrack belted 'Son of a gun, we'll have big fun, on the bayo.'

A debate on the drama took place on the RTÉ radio arts programme *Rattlebag*. On it was a man from Clogheen, who had been active during its convulsions over refugees being sent to their town, and who recognised his town and its people in the drama and was enthusiastic about the portrayal. Diarmuid Doyle of the *Sunday Tribune* heard the radio debate in a taxi with the driver agreeing with the man from Clogheen, saying, 'It must be very hard for a small town of 1500 people to suddenly have 30 baloobas living amongst them.' Possibly influenced by hearing the radio debate before viewing the drama (the vagaries of videotape!), when he came to reviewing it, he wrote:

> In trying to satirise small town Ireland and its attitude to refugees, Stembridge has provided it with a working manual on racism, a convincing and welcome reflection of its battle to save itself from the 'blackies'. One may argue that it isn't Stembridge's fault if people missed the irony and satire at the heart of his drama, but this is prime time television … it needs to be scripted … to ensure that the message of the programme is clear to the overwhelming majority of people who watch it. While some people complained at the *Fargo*-like condescension towards redneck culchies they perceived in *Black Day at Black Rock*, others clearly believed that RTÉ had provided them with a validation of their anti-refugee arguments … it came uncomfortably close to making the argument it set out to destroy … it suffered from the fact that everybody, no matter what side of the argument they were on, was a caricature.[11]

Taken one by one, character by character, declaration by declaration, each one was someone who could exist saying what could and would be said. Taken all together and juxtaposed to each other, this was the condensation that is satirical drama. The dominant point of view was that of the young people in the town, particularly the voice of one who spoke at the town meeting, open to multiplicity and adventure. The fact that the position to which the author was most opposed was mostly fully aired and done in a way that these very people

---

11 Diarmuid Doyle, *Sunday Tribune*, 4 February 2001.

recognised themselves, was to be commended. Nevertheless they were shown to engage in deception and manipulation and murder. The drama was anything but a vindication. This was cutting edge contemporary drama.

AUTUMN 2001: A NEW START?

The autumn 2001 season brought a sense of a new turn in drama for RTÉ. There was more new contemporary drama announced than for any season for a very long time. *On Home Ground*, the flagship production of the season, moved into the *Glenroe* slot. It was an eight-part serial of one-hour episodes made by Little Bird for RTÉ and set in and around a GAA club in the fictional Irish town of Kildoran. They hadn't won the county championship since 1962. After ten years of coaching without success, Fergal 'Gale Force' Collins was under pressure. It was hard to imagine that he was ever a gale force, but some characters who remembered thought so.

Critics writing after the first episode took a let's-give-it-a-chance stance. It looked well. It was in its way Ireland as we knew it. Nothing much happened, but it had a confident unhurried mood, and it established characters. Comparisons were drawn with *Ballykissangel* (*Ballykissangel* with balls), *Playing the Field* and *Dream Team*. The day after there were even reviews on the sports pages. Kevin O'Shaughnessy thought that, for all its cinematic qualities, its football was Mary Poppins gentle, passionless and pedestrian.[12] Tom Humphries said that it was a breakthrough, depicting GAA men 'as something other than hurley wielding fundamentalists with drink problems and poor dental work'.[13] Indeed, in the same paper, Hugh Linehan commented on the glossy sheen and implausibly well-groomed characters, while impressed with its picture of a quintessentially modern Ireland in a satellite boomtown on a radial route out of its capital.[14] John Boland thought that it would have to develop a dramatic pulse if we were to keep watching and in the first episode there was none.[15]

There was none in the subsequent episodes either, nor in the second series that ran in 2002. It was cool and contemporary in its way with mobile phones, camcorders, new estates, night clubbing, whatever, but it was still cozy dozy television. Characters revealed no hidden depths or even remarkable surfaces. There were some points of interest in the way it related past to present, although I found it hard to appreciate how holding up a cup in the town square all those years ago could loom so large after so many years and so many other more important things happening. I have lived a different kind of life,

12 Kevin O'Shaughnessy, *Irish Independent*, 5 November 2001.   **13** Tom Humphries, *Irish Times*, 5 November 2001.   **14** Hugh Linehan, *Irish Times*, 3 November 2001.   **15** John Boland, *Irish Independent*, 10 November 2001.

but this drama could perhaps have bridged that gap a bit. There was a scene when an older GAA activist was explaining it to a young female journalist: 'It binds the whole community together. That's the thing about sport.' Playing a tape from the time, he observed: 'The way he says their names … listen … making gods of country lads.'

In another scene, the younger generation were referring to the priest after whom Foley Field was named. One said that he was killed by the Black and Tans, while another said that he was riding a farmer's wife and the farmer had him shot. There was an intriguing back story concerning a prominent GAA family and an alienated brother whose daughter appeared as the representative of a multinational high-tech company who had the decision to make about whether the local club would be the recipient of corporate sponsorship. It was said of her father, now dead, that he hated the church and de Valera and the GAA. Why? It never came effectively into play. Perhaps I imagined it, but I thought I saw and heard a scene in a Dublin flat where RTÉ news was on and reporting the events of September 11. However, nobody said anything about it and it made the obsession with 1962 seem even more disproportionate.

Since this time, Ireland got caught up in a national-international drama (or mini-series) surrounding its participation in the world cup, both on and off the pitch. Sport obviously meets some huge human needs, but it has come to loom so large in contemporary culture and to displace so many other institutions and activities that have fulfilled and could fulfil those needs, that searching questions could be asked about it. There is such major human investment in it, economic and emotional, that needs critical probing. Television drama could contribute as much to this as academic seminars. There is more drama on this terrain these days, but it is not illuminating it to any significant degree.

The Cassidys
RTÉ was still trying to crack comedy. *The Cassidys*, a six-part sitcom by Graph Films for RTÉ, bore the burden of breaking the sitcom hex that somehow has plagued RTÉ. It didn't. It was about three orphaned siblings in their twenties sharing a suburban house. Barry was an actor who had not yet got his big break. Emma was trying to sort out the relationship of having a career to being a woman, although she had no idea what to do about men. Lisa was a UCD student trying to write a novel, only she couldn't figure out about what and how. There were some good gags for example, Barry getting so caught up with a new task scheduler that he couldn't go for an audition, because it was during his scheduled time to call around and look for auditions. However, the consensus among critics and others was that RTÉ still had not made a credible sitcom. Students were scathing about it. Indeed, there was a questioning of the sitcom genre and laugh track in favour of the comedy drama, particularly as

The Cassidys invited comparison with *Bachelor's Walk*, which was scheduled just after it.

Bachelor's Walk

Bachelor's Walk was an eight-part comedy drama made on location around Dublin on digital video with a *verité* look, an Accomplice Films production for RTÉ and BBC. It was three 30-somethings trying to find love (and sex too) in the city. Written and directed by John and Kieran Carney and Tom Hall, it was a semi-autobiographical venture.

Bachelor #1, Raymond, was a second-string film critic relegated to reviewing *Rugrats* or *Pokemon* in Dublin while the top critic was off in Cannes. He owned a crumbling townhouse on the quays, but could not squeeze rent out of his dosser housemates. His ex arrived back from the US, having moved on with her career, and he found it hard to read the signals about the nature of their relationship now. Bachelor #2, Michael, walked around dressed as a dishevelled barrister, but spent his days in pubs and bookies and rarely set foot anywhere near the courts. He risked his relationship with Jane, because she wanted to be grown up and move on and he did not. Bachelor #3, Barry, was a total chancer, seducing schoolgirls and talking absolute crap. After blowing it on the FÁS computer course, which he had to take to continue on the dole, he launched into rhetorical flight about 'vision', taking an unfortunate Croatian with him. The first step was to brainstorm, he said, to get ideas down on paper, but did they have any paper? No. They proceeded to a cyber café, where Barry asked if it could handle the overspill needs of their company. Although there was no company and the overspill was one, he enquired if there was a corporate rate. His e-mail address was bazballs@hotmail.com. Basically, none of them had been able to make the transition from university, where they were once full of promise, to an adult life. With every passing year, they were falling more and more behind. They certainly hadn't cracked the marketplace. More importantly, they hadn't quite got on track with maturity, although they occasionally made the odd foray into it.

The females in the series were a constant contrast, even the schoolgirl, much more together and moving on in life. A fourth housemate was Alison, torn between the blooming relationship with Raymond and her fiancé, a doctor in Donegal. The characters moved through Dublin, and in one episode Donegal, in a way that captured the sense of it for those who were struggling to find their way in it. It was a critical and popular success. Although the then Minister for Health, Micheál Martin, complained about the main characters smoking in it, he admitted that he had not actually seen it. It became must-see tv for those weeks. It ended with the three bachelors sitting in a room realising or half-realising how ludicrous their adult lives were, while listening to Tom

Waits singing 'Kentucky Avenue', a melancholic evocation of childhood, of male bravado and hopeful adventure:

> Let's fill our pockets with macadamia nuts
> And go over to Bobby Goodmanson's and jump off the roof ...
>
> Then we'll spit on Ronnie Arnold and flip him the bird
> And slash the tires on the school bus, now don't say a word ...
>
> I'll take the spokes from your wheelchair and a magpie's wings
> And I'll tie them to your shoulders and your feet ...

A montage of other characters appeared wistfully moving on, intercut with the three lads sitting in the living room with tears streaming down their cheeks, while Tom Waits rasped on. It was a brave and unexpected way to end what was billed as a comedy drama. Then, utterly discordantly, while the credits came up, Tom Waits was faded down and the continuity announcer chirped up that it was the end of those boys, but next week you could see another set of boys in the slot, so tune in to *Men Behaving Badly*. It had to be seen and heard to convey how clueless and out of kilter it was. The mood, so carefully constructed, was so carelessly broken. It was a weird reminder that television is not only the programme but the flow. A second and third series were subsequently aired.

Any Time Now

Moving from a core of three 30-something males to three 30-something females was *Any Time Now*, a six-part series made by Comet Films for BBCNI and RTÉ and shown in 2002. A failed actress arrived back from the USA after the death of her weatherman father, to find a wicked stepmother on the scene. An unemployed single mother decided that she wanted her husband and her job back, both in a newspaper arts section. A successful property developer, who had a job, a house, a fiancé, and who knew her way around boom town, fell into the arms of her friend's ex and fell out briefly with her friend. The city came across as up-and-coming, thrusting and vibrant, which was more than could be said of the characters, who were soft, self-obsessed and superficial, but not very interestingly so.

The authors wanted to see people like themselves on television, which was fair enough, but they failed to probe either character or milieu in a way that made the rest of us much want to see them there. The contrast, which could not entirely have been intended, between the energy and adventure of the city, and the lazy cozy schoolgirl relationship of the three main characters, somehow jarred. There were some swipes at the nasty and grasping nature of the property industry and the frothiness of the new cappuccino culture, but they seemed unable to put their finger on what was wrong with it. It did look well. The outdoor shooting of Dublin captured the dynamism of the twenty-first-century city, but scenes inside newspaper offices or television studios didn't really convey a sense of what went on there. The happy-ever-after ending, with the friends sticking together through thick and thin, and each of them getting what she wanted, was twee. It was aiming for the territory of *Cold Feet, Big Bad World* and *This Life*, but it did not arrive there. It lacked the grit, the ironic observation.

Fergus's Wedding

Fergus's Wedding was an attempt to cast an ironic eye on the more ludicrous layers of life in tiger town. Fergus from Rathfarnham, running a café called Ferguccino's and looking for romance in the personal ads and suburban swinging scene, found Penny, an English travel agent and woman of his dreams. A six-part comedy drama made by Ian Fitzgibbon and Michael McElhatton, who had delivered the semi-successful *Paths to Freedom*, it did not quite hit its target. It was generally found to be too parodic at baseline to set up parodic contrast (or something like that). It was hard to say why it didn't quite work in the way it intended. It did have its moments though. I thought that it did almost work in its own weird way. There was the running contrast between the conventional wedding being planned, according to the strictures of the old-fashioned Irish mammy and authoritarian priest who would be officiating, and the suburban swinging 'lifestyle choice' of Fergus and Penny. This truly was *à la carte* Catholicism. There were some mad scenes, such as where Fergus was explaining to Tony what was a 'mature' approach to swinging or where the tribunal judge in s & m gear regretted that he couldn't attend the wedding, because he was having a hip replacement that week. The throwaway sex talk passed without much comment from the guardians of the nation's morals. For example, Fergus responding to an overture from Penny, conceded: 'O.K., but doggy style if you don't mind, because me hip is giving me ferocious gyp.'

Where was the audience that hounded *The Spike* off the air after a mild scene of a nude model in an art class? Had the children whose teachers organised them to write letters of protest to RTÉ all grown up to be cappuccino swilling swingers or what? Had Ireland outgrown its prurient obsession with sex? Had it learned to laugh?

No Tears

There were no laughs in *No Tears*. The bleakest of the new productions, it was a thinly fictionalised account of real events in the 1990s, a four-part serial made by Little Bird and Comet for RTÉ. It opened with a montage of actuality television from the 1990s, with scenes from *RTÉ News*, *Prime Time* and *The Late Late Show*, with outraged voices and repeated phrases such as 'public health scandal' and 'human tragedy'. Then came the opening credits. After that it was back to a fictional scene of a young woman giving birth in Dublin in 1977. Then it moved to an older woman and her family on a farm in Donegal in 1986. It showed both women trying to get on with their everyday lives, but feeling very very tired. The first episode foregrounded the younger woman, who was experiencing an inexplicable and crippling fatigue, and dramatised her helplessness as her life inexorably unravelled. Both women eventually heard news via radio that suddenly explained what had seemed inexplicable.

From there subsequent episodes opened out on the lives of a number of women who discovered that they had been infected with Hepatitis C by contaminated blood products when given anti-d injections years before. It showed these women, who had been individual, alone and powerless, coming together and discovering the power of collective action. They formed a campaign group dedicated to revealing the truth and taking on the authorities. The drama traced their ups and down, their achievements and disappointments. It came to light that over a thousand women had been infected by contaminated blood products through the negligence of the Blood Transfusion Service Board. They did not just step up and demand truth and justice and get it. As if the original injustice done to them was not bad enough, many obstacles were placed in their way. The character Gráinne McFadden, recognisably Bridget McCole,[16] was forced into an unsatisfactory settlement on her deathbed. The Minister for Health, referred to as 'the minister' in the drama, obviously Michael Noonan, came out of it very badly.

There was much public discourse surrounding the drama before, during and after transmission, from talk show slots featuring Brenda Fricker (who played Gráinne McFadden) to doorstepping demands on Michael Noonan to give an account of himself. Noonan veered from ominous remarks about its legal riskiness to effusive apology to the family of Bridget McColl and other victims. Much of the talk had to do with the timing of transmission. Michael Noonan had since become leader of Fine Gael and there was a general election about to be called. As it happened, Fine Gael did very badly and Noonan resigned. While the confused position of Fine Gael within the changing ideological spectrum of Irish politics was the primary reason, it cannot be denied that this drama could have been a contributory factor. It made a story that had

---

16 Bridget McCole contracted Hepatitis C from contaminated blood products in the 1970s. Her case was the catalyst for a tribunal of inquiry chaired by Mr Justice Thomas Finlay which sat until February 1997. She died in October 1996.

already been in the public domain far more vivid in terms of specific lives injured, undermined, exhausted, terminated, bereaved.

There was no happy-ever-after ending to this drama. *No Tears* was not an obvious title for this drama. Both the events dramatised and the dramatisation of the events undoubtedly caused many tears to flow. Anyone watching the death and funeral scenes in the final episode would have been hard put to keep their eyes dry.

As long as life generates highs and lows, ironies and tragedies, television drama should provoke both laughs and tears. The new productions had both. Whatever the pluses and minuses of the 2001–2002 productions, there was a new rhythm to drama production. 'We need to get back into the swing of it', said Gerard Stembridge, 'and that needs critical mass.' In the 90s there was a tendency 'to swing from depression and harsh criticism to euphoria at something half good'.[17] The changeover in management and attitude in RTÉ augured well. The financial situation in RTÉ, with denial of the requested increase in licence fee and the general economic downturn, augured badly.

17 Interview with Gerard Stembridge, 19 August 2001.

CHAPTER 5

British production of Irish television drama

Much of the British television drama set in Ireland over the years was about the Troubles, whether historical roots or contemporary manifestations. One was called *Troubles*. This was a two-part adaptation of the novel by J.G. Farrell produced by Little Bird for LWT in 1988. It was set in 1919 and dwelt on the world of the Anglo-Irish ascendancy as their power ebbed away and the forces of republicanism threatened. Much of it was in the mood of *The Irish RM*. There was the Englishman abroad trying to come to terms with the natives: 'Surely there is no need to abandon one's reason simply because one is in Ireland?'

When reviewing it on radio, I had lost patience by this time with this sort of endless indulgence of 'big house' dottiness. It was a surreal scenario, but to what purpose? It was comic exaggeration, but it did not click as satire. It certainly communicated no sense whatsoever of what the Troubles were all about.

The Troubles dramas varied in setting, approach and point of view. Addressing the content and context of this in his doctoral thesis and later in his book *Screening Ireland*, Lance Pettitt summarised:

> Much of this fictional exposition has ... struggled in an institutional environment circumscribed by periodic direct censorship, restrictive codes of practice and a deeper cultural myopia. Unsurprisingly, television drama about Northern Ireland has tended to endorse the political status quo. On occasion the hegemonic views of political and cultural elites have been challenged, but effective interventions using drama from within influential cultural institutions such as the BBC have been intermittent, not an organised campaign by the 'Brits Out of Telly Centre'. Nor have individual programmes 'glorified the IRA' at the expense of the RUC. Nor has there been ... a 'masked posture' against the British presence in Northern Ireland. However, the creative dissidence of many writers and directors tends to lead them away from

17 Michael Sheridan as Jackie Healy Rae in *Bull Island* (2001).

18 Keith McErlean as Barry Boland, Simon Delaney as Michael Quinn and
Don Wycherley as Raymond Lawlor in *Bachelor's Walk* (2001).

19 Laura Brennan as Finn McFadden and Maria Doyle-Kennedy as Kitty
Fogarty in *No Tears* (2002).

20 Scene from *On Home Ground* (2001).

21 Scene from *Black Day at Black Rock* (2001).

22 Stuart Dunne as Billy Meehan and Lise-Ann McLaughlin as
Pauline Fitzpatrick in *Fair City* (2001).
23 Jim Bartley as Bela Doyle (*left*) and Patrick David Nolan as
Barry O'Hanlon in *Fair City* (2001).

24 Séamus Moran and Ciara O'Callaghan as
    Mike and Yvonne in *Fair City* (2001).
25 Stuart Dunne and Aisling O'Neill as Billy
    and Carol in *Fair City* (2001).

26 Julianne Moore in *Not I*, directed by Neil Jordan
in the *Beckett on Film* series (2001).

received ideas and formal political ideologies, to the possibility of imagining situations and emotions beyond mere verisimilitude, historical fact or autobiographical experience. Many ... have offered qualified questioning if not radical revisions of their cultural inheritances and political ideologies ... in some cases TV drama has pre-empted political events of the future, allowed fresh insights into the past and displayed the capacity to make people interrogate received ideas.[1]

The television drama of the Troubles did much to portray the texture of everyday life underlying the news reports and to give political ideologies a human face and voice. Looking at them chronologically: *Final Run* was a four-part BBC thriller in 1988 about a computer expert in a Belfast bank, who diverted funds to the IRA, was caught and turned informer in prison. Episodes recounted his problems with police, wife and son in setting up a new identity in England. *Crossfire*, a five-part BBC serial withdrawn in 1987,[2] was transmitted in 1988. An episode of the BBC legal series *Blind Justice* in 1988 dealt with the involvement of MI5 in an IRA case with many twists and turns of plot. *An Unreported Incident* (BBC 1988) by David Martin concentrated on a chat show host who found himself interviewing a man he shot in a border incident some years before. *Elephant* (BBC 1989) by Alan Clark was premised on the wry observation that for those living in Northern Ireland the Troubles were as easy to ignore as an elephant in your living room. It dealt with sectarian murders. *Chinese Whispers* (BBC 1989) by Maurice Leitch was about a psychiatric nurse in a mental ward and how the madness of the troubles impinged on other forms of madness. *Beyond the Pale* (BBC 1989) by William Trevor revealed the impact of the troubles on four English friends on holiday and their stereotypes of the Irish.

A *Safe House* (BBC 1990) was about the arrest of Irish people in the aftermath of the Guildford and Woolwich pub bombings in 1974 and the subsequent scapegoating of the Maguire family. Also in 1990 were ITN drama-documentaries: *Dear Sarah*, covering the same ground; *Who Bombed Birmingham?* on the Birmingham Six; and *Shoot to Kill* on the investigation into counter-terrorist activities of the RUC and MI5 covered by the never-published Stalker report. Much controversy surrounded *Shoot to Kill* and UTV did not air it.

Children of the North was a four-part BBC thriller in 1991 based on a trilogy of novels by M.S. Power. It was postponed for several months, as it was

---

1 Lance Pettitt, *Screening Ireland* (Manchester: Manchester University Press, 2000) pp. 227–8. His PhD thesis was 'A Box of Troubles' (UCD 1991). A book taking the opposite point of view is Brian McIlroy, *Shooting to Kill* (Trowbridge: Flicks, 1998).   2 Helena Sheehan, *Irish Television Drama* p. 405.

thought to be inappropriate to show undercover operations in Northern Ireland while British forces were engaged in Iraq. It showed elements within the IRA, RUC and British Army intelligence engaged in delicate peace moves and facing opposition on their own side. The IRA commander acting as go-between was murdered on the orders of the hard-line chief of staff. Nevertheless, tabloids and tories said that it was IRA propaganda.[3] *Love Lies Bleeding* by Ronan Bennett (BBC 1993) was also about a split within the IRA over ceasefire and peace moves. However, in this the pro-peace faction resorted to murder of hardliners to achieve peace, in a plot full of paradox and questions about means and ends. The play became controversial even before transmission, when it became known that Bennett, a former republican prisoner, was commissioned to write it. *Breed of Heroes* (BBC 1994) by Charles Wood, based on a novel by Alan Judd, concerned a group of British Army officers on a tour of duty in Belfast in 1971. When the heroics they expected were not required, they coped with being pelted with rocks by kids and sniped at by the IRA by retreating into the rituals of the officers' mess.

In 1994 there was an IRA ceasefire and the difficulties in the peace process were played out in drama as well as in life and on the news. *Life after Life* (BBC 1995) by Graham Reid portrayed the problems of adjustment of a republican ex-prisoner released into ceasefire Belfast after a life sentence. Instead of a hero's welcome, honouring his sacrifice, he found that life had moved on, that politics was moving to a different agenda and there seemed to be no place for him. *The Precious Blood* (BBC 1996), also by Graham Reid, turned to the dilemmas of a loyalist paramilitary prisoner who becomes a born-again 'by the power of the blood' Protestant evangelist just when he is getting to know a woman who is searching for the identity of an IRA man who killed her husband – a police informer in the UVF – while he knows that he himself was the assassin. Her traumatised son launched a frenzied attack on the local UVF headquarters and was stoned in the street to near death. It confronted difficult questions of truth and reconciliation on the ground, another dimension of the peace process, aside from official negotiations. Survivors still had to live with their losses, while knowing that the person who destroyed their lives could be passing them in the streets. *A Rap at the Door* (BBC 1999) by Pearse Elliott was also about coming to terms with the past during the peace process. Told in the form of three monologues from the children of a mother who disappeared fifteen years before, after answering a knock on the door, it was reminiscent of the fate of Jean McConville, a widowed mother of ten who was lifted by the IRA in the belief that she was an informer.

3 Edward Braun, 'What truth is there in this story? The dramatisation of Northern Ireland' in Jonathan Bignell et al. (eds.) *British Television Drama* (Basingstoke: Palgrave, 2000).

In January 2002 there were two full-scale documentary dramas marking the thirtieth anniversary of 30 January 1972, known in Ireland as Bloody Sunday. Paul Greengrass's *Bloody Sunday* zeroed in on the twenty-four hours of the event itself, focusing on Ivan Cooper MP making his rounds of the Bogside as the community made its preparations for a civil rights march. Jimmy's McGovern's *Sunday* anchored the story in the family of John Young who died that day and took the narrative forward to the denial of truth and justice that was the Widgery Tribunal. Neither probed character very deeply or created a single moment of narrative pleasure. Both were extremely effective, however, in conveying the communal tragedy of the day and its legacy. There were unforgettable scenes of mayhem in the streets, of people running, screaming, pleading, dying, grieving. There were images of pumped-up paras, matched by images of peaceful protestors in the beginning and by images of young lads taking the IRA oath of allegiance at the end.

Dealing with the Troubles and the peace process in a comic as opposed to tragic mode have been productions such as *Foreign Bodies*, a BBCNI sitcom by Bernard Farrell and Graham Reid, which went for two series in the late 80s; *Arise and Go Now* (BBC 1991) by Owen O'Neill, an alternative comedian, gave an alternative comic account of the troubles, particularly on the havoc caused by bungling IRA men in a small town; *So You Think You've Got Troubles?*, an Alomo-BBC 1991 sitcom about a London Jewish manager transferred by his company to Belfast; *Safe and Sound*, a Witzend-BBCNI six-part sitcom about the lives and loves of two garage mechanics in 1996 and *Eureka Street* (above, p. —) in 1999.

The most extended effort at Troubles/Peace Process comedy was *Give My Head Peace*, a BBCNI sitcom running since 1998. Written and performed by the zany Hole in the Wall Gang, its basic set-up was a satirical version of love across the orange and green divide. The core characters were members of two working-class families, one loyalist and the other republican, who were related through mixed marriage. The primary targets of parodic send-up were the ideologies of nationalism and unionism and lives lived under their spell. The Protestant work ethic was articulated by a loudmouthed layabout. It mocked the hollowness of much of the political discourse in various ways. Sometimes it was by using the language of political negotiation in domestic disputes, talking about 'totality of relations' and 'a three-stranded approach' to the most mundane matters. Sometimes it was by treating irreverently what was usually treated reverently, such as Ma beating John Hume off with a brush as he launched into 'his interminable single transferable speech'. The debate about the future of the police force was dealt with by having the Catholic Emer recruited into the RUC under pressure to reform its ranks in terms of both religious affiliation and gender, her being rapidly promoted to chief constable and going on an authoritarian power-trip, even arresting Mo Mowlam, secretary of state, for having an out-of-date car tax disk.

The series assumed a high degree of intertextual reference, not only to the politics of the North in news and current affairs discourse, but to a wide range of literary, theatrical, cinematic and televisual genres. The names of episodes, for example, assumed knowledge of numerous texts: 'Saving Ryan's Daughter', 'Luke Back in Anger', 'The Talented Mr Ripple', 'The Importance of Being Protestant', 'The Sectarian Candidate', 'Bonfire of the Insanities'. The episode on Emer in the RUC was done in the style of the ITN police series *The Bill*. In another episode, Andy and his orange friend set out to march on Ballykissangel, the name of a fictional village in another BBCNI series. 'Taking on Hollywood', another episode, had an American actor arrive to research the role of Gerry Adams, despite being blond, beardless and utterly unable to master a Belfast accent. It undermined the old Northern Ireland and implicitly hoped to be clearing the ground for the new.

As the Beast Sleeps, adapted from the Gary Mitchell play, was a BBC production described as having the dimensions of Greek tragedy and set in the climate following the Good Friday agreement centring on a gunman forced to choose between old loyalties and new realities.

Not all the British production of television drama set in Ireland dealt with the troubles. *The Temptation of Eileen Hughes* was an adaptation of a Brian Moore story by BBC in 1988. *Last of a Dyin' Race*, a UTV comedy by Christina Reid in 1988, concerned the clash of old and new in the way of funeral customs. It dealt with separation of the sexes and the effect of class and upward mobility. *Monkeys* (BBCNI 1989) was a Paul Muldoon play about the life and arrest of businessman John DeLorean. *The Hen House* (BBCNI 1989) was a Frank McGuinness play about a woman keeping to herself on a smallholding in Donegal, who got caught up in a game of hide-and-seek and exposure of secrets. *The Englishman's Wife* (BBCNI 1990) by Holly Chandler was about a mother and daughter in poor economic circumstances in County Tyrone. *August Saturday* (BBCNI 1990) was a William Trevor story of a group of friends who met once a month for dinner and the impact of the return of a friend who hadn't attended in fifteen years.

All Things Bright and Beautiful (BBCNI 1994) by Barry Devlin was about a 10-year-old altar boy subject to power of suggestion and seeing visions. *Runway 1* by Barry Devlin was a two-part thriller about a pair of Irish policemen caught up in an international conspiracy involving sex, guns, drugs and beef. *Loving* (BBCNI 1996) was an upstairs-downstairs big house drama set in 1941, based on the Henry Green novel. *A Man of No Importance* (BBCNI 1996) by Barry Devlin was about a bus conductor reciting Oscar Wilde in

Dublin in the 1960s. *Vicious Circle* (BBCNI 1999) by Kieran Prendiville, was another Martin Cahill biopic.

Sinners (BBCNI 2002) was set in one of the horrific Magdalen laundries of past decades, where girls who 'got into trouble' were sent to give birth, do penance and provide free labour under the authority of sometimes sadistic nuns. The inequality of treatment of males and females who transgressed was sharply highlighted. The central character, Anne Marie, gave birth to the son of herself and her brother. He prospered while she was punished. The mental and physical suffering of such young women was credibly conveyed.

There were also a number of series of short dramas going under the umbrella of *Northern Lights* made by independent production companies for BBCNI. Some of these were also shown on RTÉ in its *Debut* slot.

Ballykissangel

Ballykissangel was a BBCNI comedy series running from 1996 to 2001. It was set in the south rather than the north, and its humour was more whimsical than satirical. A picturesque production made in County Wicklow, created by Kieran Prendiville, it deployed a fine Irish cast on Irish soil to create a foreign fantasy of Irish life. It opened with the arrival of an English priest destined to play straight man to the many crafty Irish locals. It was supposed to be contemporary, and indeed in many ways it was, to gauge it by fax machines, satellite dishes, mobile phones and websites, but other things about it set it decades back. It wasn't just the obvious things, such as priests wearing roman collars and black suits and being central to village life as well as old biddies and scheming gombeens and comely colleens and devious boyos. It was the will o' the wisp feel to it, the warm and witty gentility of it, that harkened back, not so much to real village life of previous time, but a Hollywood version of it. As the *Irish Times* review characterised it:

> *Ballykissangel* will do nothing to break the thought patterns of the English towards the Irish. Set in an Irish village that's about 40 years behind *Glenroe*, it's super-light in a heavy-handed sort of way. Avoca, starring as the village of the title, looks splendid, but the roguish eccentrics are unbelievable. This is *Son of Darby O'Gill* country with generous measures of *The Quiet Man* and *Finian's Rainbow*, just to be sure, to be sure … There is an irritating jauntiness … It might be justifiable, if it were hilariously funny, but it's not … this is cozy drama for the contented.[4]

---

4 Eddie Holt, *Irish Times*, 16 February 1996.

Such tended to be the attitude to it in Ireland, but it was much more highly rated in Britain, America and elsewhere. It proved a winner for the BBC, not only of awards, but in international sales. It seemed to correspond to an Ireland of the imagination for much of the world. The stereotypes were not way over the top or obnoxious, but more gentle and playful. It was in its way very well made. It evolved through several series, as various characters and writers came and went. It became somewhat more serious for a while, particularly with the deaths of Assumpta and then Ambrose. It also had declarations of unbelief in God from core characters, such as Assumpta and Brian.

Catholicism was central to the series, but was not taken very seriously by it. It was a source of laughs basically, starting with the air-conditioned fax-equipped confessional in series 1 to the confession online website in series 6 and many other gags in between. When the new Aussie priest came across a shrine, the garda commented: 'It doesn't move apparently'. A revealing bit of dialogue in divulging the stance of the series itself came when the Aussie priest asked the local kid why he set up the confession website in the *God.com* episode:

— Fr Vincent Sheehan: I didn't think that this was such a religious country any more.
— Dermot Dooley: It's not, but the yanks still think it is.

Father Ted

If *BallyK* found Catholicism to be mildly funny, then *Father Ted* found it hilarious. Created by Graham Linehan and Arthur Mathews and produced by Hat Trick for Channel 4, *Father Ted* ran from 1995 to 1998. It has often been said, even written in newspapers, that RTÉ turned down *Father Ted*, but the fact is that it was never offered it. It was subsequently shown on RTÉ, and it was enormously popular in Ireland, whether seen on Channel 4 or RTÉ or both.

It was set in a parochial house on the fictional Craggy Island in a real-surreal Ireland. In this house, full of Catholic kitsch, lived three priests and their housekeeper and through it trooped many more priests, bishops, nuns, pop stars, parishioners and lots of rabbits, all of them weird and wonderful caricatures. Father Ted himself, masterfully and manically played by Dermot Morgan, was a middle-aged smart-ass cynic, who had been banished to Craggy Island for financial irregularities, something to do with money raised to send a sick child to Lourdes 'only resting' in Ted's own account. Father Jack Hackett, much older, had obviously been sent to the outer reaches of church life because he was an alcoholic and reprobate. Father Dougal McGuire, much younger, seemed not to understand even the most basic tenets of Catholic theology, but had somehow become a priest. At times he asked Ted, quite innocently, if he believed in God or if he believed in an afterlife, and responded: 'Gee, I wish I had your faith, Ted.' Whatever his offence was, it had caused irreparable damage to several nuns. He had a shirt that said: 'It's a priest thing. You wouldn't understand.'

Mrs Doyle meanwhile tended to their every need, especially with tea and egg sandwiches and Ferraro Rochers. At one stage, she was even giving Father Dougal a bath. The activities of the priests were multifarious and often mad: compering a 'lovely girls competition', picketing a blasphemous film (thus giving it unprecedented popularity), entering the Eurovision Song Contest, getting trapped in a lingerie department.

In an episode entitled *Tentacles of Doom*, they received a letter announcing that the holy stone of Clonrichert was to be upgraded to a class-2 relic and that no less than three bishops would be arriving for the ceremony. Ted was worried about the impression Jack might make and undertook to coach him to say something other than 'drink', 'feck' or 'girls' and to say, in answer to any question, 'That would be an ecumenical matter', confessing that he often said that when he didn't know what else to say, and observing: 'That's the great thing about Catholicism. It's so vague that nobody really knows what it's about.'

When the bishops arrived, they each ranted on their favourite topic, such as the role of the laity or anticlerical bias in the media: 'You can barely open a newspaper these days without reading some anticlerical article by some bearded leftie ...' On the way back from the ceremony, each of the bishops engaged in conversation with one of the priests on his pet theme. Bishop O'Neill asked Dougal if he ever had any doubts. At first Dougal did not know what he meant. The bishop pressed him. Then Dougal started listing the things he found hard to believe: 'You know the way God made us all, right? and he's looking down from heaven and everything? and then his son came down and saved everyone and all that? ... and when we die we're all going to go to heaven? That's the bit I have trouble believing in.' Suddenly the bishop started to wonder if any of it made any sense. Meanwhile, another bishop was going on about his heart attack and how it made him think about death, and the other was still ranting about the media. Back to Dougal: 'So, if God existed forever, what did he do with all that time, like before he made the earth and everything?' The bishop was stumped. By the time they reached the parochial house, Bishop O'Neill announced that he had reached some interesting conclusions:

— It's all nonsense, isn't it?
— What is?
— Religion ... I've been struggling for some time, but Father McGuire clarified the whole thing for me. God, heaven, hell ... it's all a load of rubbish ... everlasting life and big demons with hot pokers, I don't think so.

Crediting Dougal with this revelation, he told Ted: 'This man, treasure him, Father Crilly, he has wisdom far beyond his years.' A few minutes later, Bishop O'Neill had become 'Eddie' and was wearing jeans and waistcoat with a bandana around his head. A van full of hippies arrived to pick him up to go off to India. Meanwhile, Bishop Jordan had died of a heart attack and was taken out in a coffin, and Bishop Facks was taken to hospital to have the holy stone removed from where Father Jack had shoved it. At the end of it all, Ted said to Dougal: 'Went pretty well, I thought.'

When I first saw the first episode, I have to admit, I did not think that it worked. It seemed more slapstick than satire. It seemed to be too far over the top in its exaggeration to be intelligently parodic. However, once I had become more attuned to the characters and the set-up, I began to find it very funny. Not only that, but I found each episode even funnier on second or third viewing. Perhaps because priests had been treated with such reverence, it had to go in hard and create a menagerie of mad caricatures to get across how crazy a creature a priest was.

> — Dougal: God, I've heard about those cults, Ted. People dressing up in black and saying our lord's going to come back and save us all.
> — Ted: No, Dougal, That's us. That's Catholicism.
> — Dougal: Oh right.

On another occasion:

> — Ted: I'm not a fascist. I'm a priest. Fascists dress up in black and tell people what to do, whereas priests …

In every episode, there were multiple ironies. When Father Jack died, a nun at the wake was gushing to a black priest about the wonderful level of commitment of the African church, to which he said: 'Sure, I wouldn't know. I'm from Donegal.' When Dougal was asked to perform the last rites, he confessed that he didn't know how, but then decided to wing it: 'Of course, you're up there now with Our Lord and Stalin and Bob Marley and my own parents … Hello mammy and daddy.' When they were picketing a forbidden film, thus giving it unprecedented popularity, their sign read: 'Down with this type of thing.'

There were many references to Irish culture in the 1990s. When Dougal kept calling Ted 'ya big bollox' or 'ya big gobshite', Ted demanded to know: 'Dougal, have you been reading those Roddy Doyle books again?' The revelations about Bishop Eamonn Casey were mirrored in a story about Bishop Brennan, showing him cavorting on a beach with his lover and son while wearing the full ceremonial robes of a bishop. One visitor to Craggy Island was an Irish feminist pop star modelled on Sinead O'Connor. She referred to scandals over paedophile priests, and Ted reassured her: 'Well, we're not all like that, Niamh. Say, if there's 200 million priests in the world and 5% of them are paedophiles, that's still only 10 million.'

Lest anyone think that Catholicism should not be treated as farce, here the reality subsequently outstripped the fiction, when Sinead O'Connor was ordained a priest in Lourdes, renamed Mother Bernadette and announced that anyone who wanted her to perform liturgies should contact her record label. This was even more bold than any of the stream of boring priests or scheming priests or adolescent delinquent priests or manically talking, singing, dancing priests who flowed through this series.

The series was controversial, but more abroad than in Ireland. Some Irish emigrants wrote in the *Irish Post* that it was disrespectful to clergy, degrading to Irish people generally and pandered to British stereotypes of the Irish for profit.[5] Defending it against such criticisms, Lance Pettitt argued that it was a measure of Irish self-confidence that it could take the stereotypes of the coloniser, repossess and explode them. It also provided a release for the resentment Catholics felt toward the church in the wake of a wave of clerical scandals. Addressing the various readings of the show:

> The culturally specific vernacular of *Father Ted* could not only be misread by English viewers – reinforcing existing prejudices – but by first and second generation Irish viewers in Britain and the USA who held simplistic notions of how popular media stereotypes circulate. Such complainants failed to see that there were alternative approaches to positive imaging ... The divisiveness of *Father Ted* is ludic, tracing the shifting contours of postcolonial representation and reinscribing the boundaries of social conflict. It shows how media texts become meaningful in ways that are dependent upon specific combinations of residual and emergent representations, and particular cultural cross-overs being interpreted at any given time by situated audiences within and without Ireland.[6]

There has always been sensitivity about representation of Irishness for foreign audiences. There was a kind of stage Irishry to it, but it was a knowing kind. Indeed, it was stage Irishness itself being satirised.

---

5 *Irish Post*, 6 April, 20 May 1995, cited by Lance Pettitt, op. cit., pp. 196, 204. Pettitt also cited views of academics in America and Australia in an Irish studies e-mail discussion group in January 1998.
6 Ibid.

It was more controversial for its representation of Catholicism than of nationality, but only in America were objections to it able to exert any real pressure. There was disquiet among traditional Catholics and their clergy. In Ireland, it was muted, reflecting the decline in the cultural power and moral authority of the church. There was no way they were in a position to mount the sort of pressure on RTÉ (much less Channel 4) that they could in previous decades (as recounted in my earlier book).[7] When you think of the furore caused by the nude scene in *The Spike* and then think of scenes in *Father Ted*, including a priest in a bathtub being bathed by his housekeeper and a bishop and priest waking up nude in bed together, you get a sense of how much had changed. A lot of Catholics, including priests, said that they liked it, that it was healthy and well-intended.

An American Jesuit, who discovered it in the schedule when in Britain, asked about it in his order and was told it was 'a silly piece of rubbish'. He watched it, enjoyed it and wrote a thesis on it, which included audience research among priests.[8] There were various shades of negativity, but the response, especially among his fellow Jesuits, was overwhelmingly negative. The author, Steve Baird SJ, took a positive view, believing that priests had to learn something from it, as it was so popular, particularly among the younger audience. He admitted that he found it both funny and frightening to recognise types of priests he had known.

Such an effort to be open-minded and to have a sense of humour and to be self-critical was fine, but it was open to question as to how far it faced up to the extreme alienation from Catholicism characterising the programme and its audience. The dominant point of view was that of lapsed Catholics. Like much satire, it could be appreciated at different levels, but the maximal appreciation of its humour depended on simultaneous familiarity with Catholicism and pleasure in seeing what was once a matter for absolute reverence being treated irreverently and parodied. It might have been another sitcom about priests and their housekeeper, but it could hardly have been more different than *Leave It to Mrs O'Brien*.

Of those working on the programme most were lapsed Catholics. Of writers and core cast, only Frank Kelly, who played Father Jack, was a practising Catholic. Dermot Morgan often described himself as 'a severely lapsed Catholic'. Whatever about the more benign interpretations put on it by others, Morgan did not believe that it should not offend.[9] He had grown up Catholic in Ireland and even considered being a priest. He popped up as

---

7 H. Sheehan, op.cit., pp. 84–5, 172–4.   **8** Steve Baird SJ, *A Televisual Representation of Roman Catholic Priests: Father Ted* at gabrielmedia.org/frted/.   **9** *RTÉ Guide* report on press conference on the third series of *Father Ted*.

Father Brian Trendy on *The Live Mike* satirising liberal priests. His anger at the church grew with the years and he was severely alienated from it.[10] Much of the energy of his portrayal came from his anger and alienation. He meant the satire to bite.

When he died suddenly in 1998, just as the third series of *Father Ted* had been produced but not yet transmitted, he was mourned by the nation in a way that was more genuine than for any public figure in my memory. He was embraced by the church as a wayward child. Michael Paul Gallagher SJ, who had been his teacher at UCD, did at least acknowledge the irony in his homily. Steve Baird SJ wrote: 'Dermot Morgan and Father Ted will live on in our hearts. Morgan is now with the God he was so troubled by ... please pray for us left behind.'[11] Everyone must come to terms with loss in his own way and according to his or her own world view, but the dissidence of Dermot Morgan was too neatly rehabilitated into the conventional. As I attended his funeral and listened to the prayers said over him in Glasnevin, I did not believe that he would have approved of the easy assimilation.

By now Father Ted as a character (as well as a series) and Dermot Morgan as a performer have achieved cult status. He is an icon of iconoclasm. Of all the television drama set in Ireland, perhaps ever, this has etched itself deepest in folk memory, both nationally and internationally. It has created a population of archetypal characters and points of ongoing communal reference. It has resonated as myth in the way that television sometimes can.

Adding to its afterlife, there are books, videotapes, dvds and websites.[12] In these years world wide web has been a burgeoning medium of popular culture with multiple interactions with other media, including television. Type *Father Ted* into a search engine and see how many webpages pop up. All around the world there are tedheads, who continue the cult of this series.

The Ambassador

Back to BBC Northern Ireland, which proved such a prolific producer of Irish television drama in the 1990s, another ambitious project was *The Ambassador*. This was a series built around the life and work of a British ambassador to Ireland, billed (by its producers) as the 'television event of the year' (1998). It was filmed on location in Dublin 'set in the most vibrant city in Europe'.[13] This was the capital city of Celtic tiger Ireland. Indeed, the streetscapes, parks and harbours of Dublin rarely looked more enticing.

---

10 I had a number of conversations with Dermot Morgan about politics, media and religion in the 1990s. He was seriously angry as well as very funny.   11 Baird, op. cit.   12 Graham Linehan and Arthur Mathews, *Father Ted: the Complete Scripts* (London: Boxtree, 1999). The first and second series are now available in DVD format. There are very many websites, most of them set up by fans, featuring *Father Ted*. These provide episode guides, sound files of favourite quotes and exchange of memories about the show.   13 *The Ambassador* publicity brochure.

It was very much a peace process drama in the whole mood of the series, as well as in the plots and patterns of resolution. There was an atmosphere of respect and co-operation between the two countries, whatever tensions arose when national interests were in conflict. The politics of it was vague in the sense that the governments of Britain and Ireland were not very explicitly delineated in either party or ideological terms. Nevertheless the ideological centre of gravity of the series was strongly centrist in every way, very much in tune with the mood of the times. The Irish Foreign Minister Kevin Flaherty (Owen Roe) locked horns with the British ambassador in every episode where events made it inevitable: an Irish trawler sunk (accidentally) by a British submarine, ownership of Rockall, competition for commercial contracts, loyalist versus republican ideologies playing themselves out in Northern Ireland. Their relationship was forthright and pragmatic and compromise was always on the cards. When Flaherty pleaded: 'I'm asking you to go beyond: never apologise; never explain', chances were that she would. Both were tough but fair, more or less. In the original proposal, the Irish foreign minister was to be an 'unprincipled rogue',[14] whereas by the time it came to air, his character was drawn very much like that of the British ambassador, matched in every way, allowing for differences of gender, class and nationality. The BBC was being more careful here than it was with the *EastEnders* episodes set in Ireland in autumn 2000, when the BBC apologised for any offence to Irish viewers after an outcry from critics and audience against timeworn caricatures of Ireland and the Irish, showing the Fowlers and Beales immediately encountering drunken brawling, cluelessness, livestock on the streets, slower pace of life, virtually every old cliché.

There was also the woman-in-a-man's-world angle. The ambassador was Harriet Smith, ably played by Pauline Collins, a formidable professional woman as well as the mother of two sons. There were usually subplots involving her family life and potential conflicts between her professional and personal life, but very often these were resolved in a way that that personal angle illuminated the professional or vice versa. Sometimes she seemed like a wonder woman, speaking six languages (including Arabic, Japanese and Russian), mastering details of international law, resolving the trickiest of diplomatic dilemmas, foiling devious plots of spies and civil servants, speaking sympathetically to ordinary citizens and being a caring mother. It was not all tied up unproblematically however. Indeed the back story was that her husband was killed by a car bomb in the Middle East meant for her. Her older son Nate, who was 'reading' politics at Trinity, had not forgiven her for this

---

14 I am grateful to my DCU colleague Patrick Kinsella, who was a script consultant on the series, for access to series documents and scripts.

and was constantly creating difficulties for her over it. Her positioning was articulated in a conversation between two MI6 operatives:

> — Stone: Just don't underestimate the ambassador. She's her own person.
> — Milburn: She's her country's person. That's why she's here.

In each of the 12 episodes in the two series of 1998 and 1999, the interweaving of subplots was intricate and skilful. There were often individuals in distress: a British wife of a Saudi diplomat seeking refuge, a girl framed for drug smuggling, her secretary held hostage, her mentor dying, her deputy accused of murder, her lover kidnapped, her sons feeling neglected. These were counterbalanced, not only with other short-term diplomatic exigencies, but with long-term political and commercial interests of several nations, as well as fundamental moral choices. There was an attempt to see all the world in a grain of sand in these stories. The resolutions often involved considerable intellectual and moral ambiguity:

> — Smith: The world's a confused place. I can't make it any clearer. We stumble through never really sure who the bad guys are, desperate to make things black and white. They never are.

Sometimes it seemed smug, not so much when plot resolutions were pat as when they were not, when there seemed to be a complacency about centrist ambiguity. There was talk about telling the truth and doing the right thing. There was questioning of whether ends justified means. This level of discourse was generally raised and left hanging.

It did deal with difficult issues, such as that of the British nuclear industry and its responsibility for high levels of radioactivity in the Irish Sea and consequent deaths of Irish citizens. There were two alternative episodes written surrounding the death of a child with leukaemia. In the one that was chosen, a grief-stricken father from County Louth broke into the embassy and held a secretary hostage, demanding that the British government take responsibility and close the nuclear plant in Cumbria. The alternative episode, written but not made, had the ambassador arriving at the embassy to a silent protest of an eerie procession of blown-up photos of leukaemia victims. A case in the European Court had just fallen through a loophole and fell on technical grounds. The father of a dying child joined with a Greenpeace-type of group and boarded a British merchant vessel with processed nuclear fuel on board. At a dinner party in the embassy taking place at the same time, Flaherty refused the prawns saying, 'I wouldn't eat those. Make you glow in the dark.'

Also in this episode he was telling of his trip to Brussels during the week: 'The place is totally bloody Kafka, full of low flyers, all somewhere between 40 and death. They miss Mrs Thatcher swinging her handbag in there.'

In another episode, she was prevailed upon by an MI6 operative to intervene when her former mentor was about to publish his memoirs. The dialogue was hard hitting:

> — Beauchamp: I've had an exciting privileged life … But then again, one could argue that I've spent most of it, a good 40 years, colluding with the powers of darkness.
> — Smith: Isn't that a rather harsh description?
> — Beauchamp: I'm serious … I've done my duty, but by definition that duty has often entailed moral compromise, economy with the truth, even outright denial of it.
> — Smith: Whereas now you believe that truth is everything?
> — Beauchamp: What I feel is an overwhelming need to atone in some way for my past sins of omission and acquiescence by, yes, setting the truth free. No more secrets. No more lies. Tell it like it really was. My conscience nags me with a forthright question, Harriet. What end has my 40 years of diplomacy actually achieved? Is the world a better place?
> — Smith: Surely we're trying to stop it being a worse place.
> — Beauchamp: I see no evidence that I've achieved even that limited objective. Have you?
> — Smith: I like to think so.
> — Beauchamp: So did I. It was a delusion.

There was also the voice of MI6 in this episode:

> Decisions, choices, are made, moral choices, appalling choices, and yes, they are made in secret. The war against terrorism is not a cliché. It's a fact, and in fighting it, one has to be as ruthless as the terrorists themselves. Fight fire with fire. Or be consumed.

As this book was being written, the war against terrorism came to centre stage in an unscheduled global drama.

Conclusion

When I concluded *Irish Television Drama: A Society and Its Stories* in 1987, I believed that there had been a sharp debate about television drama that I hoped had cleared the way for drama that would deal with dilemmas at the cutting edge of contemporary experience, drama that would stop ending up in conventional cul de sacs. On the whole, such hopes were disappointed. Much of what came was more of the same: too derivative, too myopic, too mundane. It was trying too little, then trying too hard, without being clear enough about what it was trying to do.

However, there was drama that tracked the tiger. There was drama that stimulated critical reflection on the path our society was pursuing, such as *The Truth About Claire, Family, Black Day at Black Rock, No Tears, Bachelor's Walk,* sometimes even *Fair City,* and in its own weird and wonderful way *Father Ted.* There was also drama that scrutinised the past in a way that assimilated it more honestly into our present: *A Love Divided, Sinners, Amongst Women.*

There were enormous changes in the mode of production of television drama, which created much of the uncertainty and disorientation, but there were deeper reasons for such confusion too. There was a postmodernist paralysis in conceptualising contemporary experience. This was a global trend and Ireland moved to global rhythms as never before.

Nevertheless, different ways of seeing the world and doing drama emerged from the vortex and made television drama that shed light on what it was to be standing in Ireland looking at the world as it emerged into the twenty-first century.

RTÉ television drama productions, 1962–1986

Abbreviations: d. = director / a. = author / p. = producer.

1962 Head of Drama 1961–1964: Hilton Edwards

Thirst
d. Sheelah Richards
a. Myles na Gopaleen

The Well of the Saints
d. Michael Hayes
a. John Millington Synge

Come Back
d. Chloe Gibson
a. Brian and Veronica Cleeve

Moby Dick Rehearsed
d. Michael Hayes
a. Herman Melville
adapted by Orson Welles

The Little Father
5 episodes
d. Peter Collinson
a. Laurence Houseman
adapted by Carolyn Swift

Hello Out There
d. Chloe Gibson
a. William Saroyan

Siopa an Bhreathnaigh
serial
d. Chloe Gibson
Gerard Victory
Michael Hayes
Peter Collinson
a. Niall Toibin

Everyman
d. Michael Hayes
*based on a 15th century
Dutch morality play*

Oliver of Ireland
      d. Sheelah Richards
      a. Frank D'Arcy

The Shewing up of Blanco Posnet
      d. Chloe Gibson
      a. George Bernard Shaw

Public Enemy
      d. Jim Fitzgerald
      a. Henrik Ibsen
       adapted by Eoin Neeson
       from **Enemy of the People**

The Bomb
      d. Peter Collinson
      a. James Douglas

The Moon Shines on Kylenamoe
      d. Sheelah Richards
      a. Sean O'Casey

Our Representative Will Call
      d. Peter Collinson
      a. Orson Welles

Heart to Heart
      d. Michael Hayes
      a. Terence Rattigan

A Matter of Conscience
      d. Sheelah Richards
      a. Eugene McCabe

1963

The Liar
      d. Michael Hayes
      a. Micheál MacLiammóir

The Glass Murder
      d. Peter Collinson
      a. Denis Johnston

The Paddy Pedlar
      d. Jim Fitzgerald
      a. M. J. Molloy

Enquiry at Lisieux
      d. Chloe Gibson
      a. Marcelle Maurette

The Long Sorrow
      d. Sheelah Richards
      a. Thomas Coffey

The Weaver's Grave
      d. Christopher FitzSimon
      a. Seamus O'Kelly
       adapted by Micheál Ó hAodha

Down at Flannery's
 serial
      d. Bill Skinner
      a. Carolyn Swift

An Apple a Day	*d.* Christopher FitzSimon
	a. Jules Romains
	adapted by Micheál MacLiammóir

The Devil a Saint Would Be — *d.* Sheelah Richards
a. Louis D'Alton
adapted by Carolyn Swift

Triptych — *d.* Jim Fitzgerald

The Workhouse Ward — *a.* Lady Gregory

In the Train — *a.* Frank O'Connor

Purgatory — *a.* W. B. Yeats

The Old Ladies — *d.* Chloe Gibson
a. Hugh Walpole
adapted by Rodney Ackland

Carrie — *d.* Peter Collinson
a. James Douglas
adapted by Wesley Burrowes
and Michael Coffey

A Walk on the Water — *d.* Jim Fitzgerald
a. Hugh Leonard

Dr. Korczak and the Children — *d.* Chloe Gibson
a. Erwin Sylvanus
adapted by Adrian Vale

She Stoops to Conquer — *d.* Chloe Gibson
a. Oliver Goldsmith

1964 *Head of Drama 1964-1965: Jim Fitzgerald*

Tolka Row
serial
n.b. The listing of directors and
authors relates to the entire run
of the programme, up to 1968.

d. Christopher FitzSimon
Peter Kennerley
Brian MacLochlainn
Jim Fitzgerald
Michael Bogdanov
a. Maura Laverty
Norman Smythe
James Douglas
Michael Judge
Lee Dunne
Colin Bird

The Chair	*d.* Peter Collinson
	a. Michael Judge
Three Fathers, Three Sons	*d.* Peter Collinson
	a. Brian Friel
In the Shadow of the Glen	*d.* Louis Lentin
	a. John M. Synge
Echoland	*d.* Louis Lentin
	a. James Joyce
	extracts from **Finnegans Wake**
Don't Ever Talk to Clocks	*d.* Peter Collinson
	a. Michael Judge
Them	*d.* Chloe Gibson
	a. Thomas Coffey
The Importance of Being Oscar	*d.* Chloe Gibson
	a. Micheál MacLiammóir
The Man of Destiny	*d.* Sheelah Richards
	a. George Bernard Shaw
The Truth about Pyecraft	*d.* Jim Fitzgerald
	a. H. G. Wells
	adapted by Douglas Clevendon
The Bear	*d.* Jim Fitzgerald
	a. Anton Chekov
Lost Property	*d.* Peter Collinson
	a. Reginald Martin
	adapted by Eoin Neeson
Anyone Can Rob a Bank	*d.* Chloe Gibson
	a. Thomas Coffey
The Duke in Darkness	*d.* Jim Fitzgerald
	a. Patrick Hamilton
The Shed	*d.* Peter Collinson
	a. Maisie Mosco
Dublin 1	*d.* Louis Lentin
	a. James Joyce
	adapted by Hugh Leonard
	from **Dubliners**

All the King's Horses	*d.* Jim Fitzgerald
	a. John McDonnell
A Letter from the General	*d.* Christopher Fitz-Simon
	a. Maurice McLoughlin
Some Women on the Island	*d.* Chloe Gibson
	a. Eugene McCabe
Mr. Power's Purchase	*d.* Sheelah Richards
	a. Brigid K. Nalton
	adapted by Eugene McCabe
I Must be Talking to My Friends	*d.* Chloe Gibson
	a. Micheál MacLiammóir
The Moon in the Yellow River	*d.* Sheelah Richards
	a. Denis Johnston
You Never Can Tell	*d.* Chloe Gibson
	a. George Bernard Shaw
Do You Know the Milky Way	*d.* Michael Lindsay-Hogg
	a. Karl Wittlinger

1965 *Head of Drama 1965-1971: Chloe Gibson*

Tolka Row
 serial

See page 105.

The Riordans
 serial
n.b. The listing of directors and
authors relates to the entire run
of the programme, up to 1979.

d. Christopher Fitz-Simon
 Sheelah Richards
 Deirdre Friel
 Tony Barry
 Brian MacLochlainn
 Louis Lentin
a. James Douglas
 Wesley Burrowes
 Joe O'Donnell
 Frank Carney
 M. J. Molloy
 Eugene McCabe
 Carolyn Swift
 Adrian Vale
 David Hanly
 Derry Power

	Thomas Coffey
	G. P. Gallivan
The Whiteheaded Boy	*d.* Jim Fitzgerald
	a. Lennox Robinson
Dawn Chorus	*d.* Louis Lentin
	a. Seán Dunne
The Hollow Field	*d.* Christopher Fitz-Simon
	a. James Douglas
An Triail	*d.* Michael Garvey
	a. Mairéad Ni Ghrada
Yesterday Is Over	*d.* Chloe Gibson
	a. Gerry Simpson
The Costigan Brothers	*d.* Jim Fitzgerald
	a. Alberto Colantioni
	adapted by Wesley Burrowes
	from **The Castiglioni**
Saighdiurí	*d.* Michael Garvey
	a. Donal MacAmhlaigh
The Scythe and the Sunset	*d.* Chloe Gibson
	a. Denis Johnston
Full Fathom Five	*d.* Louis Lentin
	a. Michael Judge
Two's Company	*d.* Louis Lentin
	a. Gilman Noonan
Danger, Men Working	*d.* Christopher Fitz-Simon
	a. John D. Stewart
	adapted by Adrian Vale
Martine	*d.* Chloe Gibson
	a. Jean-Jacques Bernard
Deirdre	*d.* Michael Garvey
	a. W.B. Yeats
The King of Friday's Men	*d.* Louis Lentin
	a. M. J. Molloy
	adapted by M. J. Molloy
	and Adrian Vale

The Year of the Hiker	*d.* Louis Lentin
	a. John B. Keane
Mourn the Ivy Leaf	*d.* Jim Fitzgerald
	a. G. P. Gallivan
A Ship in the Night	*d.* Chloe Gibson
	a. Thomas Coffey
Church Street	*d.* Sheelah Richards
	a. Lennox Robinson
The Fiend at my Elbow	*d.* Chloe Gibson
	a. Michael Judge
Autumn Fire	*d.* Jim Fitzgerald
	a. T. C. Murray
	adapted by Adrian Vale
Diplomatic Incident	*d.* Sheelah Richards
	a. W. A. Tyler
Th' Oul Lad of Kilsalahen	*d.* Jim Fitzgerald
	a. Myles na Gopaleen

1966

Tolka Row serial	*See page 105.*
The Riordans serial	*See page 107.*

The Long Winter
 – *The Great O'Neill*
 – *RememberLimerick*
 – *When do You Die, Friend?*
 – *The Greatest Son*
 – *The Uncrowned King*
 – *The Origins of the Rising*
	d. James Plunkett
	   Jim Fitzgerald
	 a. John O'Donovan
	   James Plunkett

Beginning to End	*d.* Chloe Gibson
	a. Samuel Beckett
The Bicycle Man *A Boy at the Train*	*d.* Christopher Fitz-Simon *a.* Bryan McMahon

The School on the Green
Children of Dreams
  Series of four plays for
  young viewers

Insurrection
  8 episodes
	d. Louis Lentin
	  Michael Garvey
	a. Hugh Leonard

The Siege of the Widow Wilkins	*d.* Jim Fitzgerald *a.* Rex Mackey
The Plough and the Stars	*d.* Lelia Doolan *a.* Seán O'Casey *adapted by* Blanaid Irvine
Cuirt an Mhean-Oiche	*d.* Louis Lentin *a.* Brian Merriman
An Fear Faire	*d.* Donall Farmer *a.* Padraig Ó Siochru

The Real Charlotte
  8 episodes
	d. Michael Garvey
	a. Somerville and Ross
	  adapted by Adrian Vale *and*
	  Norman Smythe

Dear Liar	*d.* Chloe Gibson
	a. George Bernard Shaw *and*
	  Mrs. Patrick Campbell
	  adapted by Jerome Kilty

Babby Joe	*d.* Chloe Gibson *a.* James Douglas
An Fear Suil	*d.* Brian MacLochlainn *a.* Lady Gregory

1967

Tolka Row *serial*	*See page 105.*
The Riordans *serial*	*See page 107.*
O Duill *8 episodes*	*d.* Donall Farmer *a.* Michael Judge

The Nigh School of Sholom Aleichem	*d.* Sheelah Richards *a.* Arnold Perl
Breakdown	*d.* Chloe Gibson *a.* Eugene McCabe
Candida	*d.* Christopher Fitz-Simon *a.* George Bernard Shaw
The Shadow of a Gunman	*d.* James Plunkett *a.* Seán O'Casey
One for the Grave	*d.* Louis Lentin *a.* Louis MacNeice
Shadows in the Sun	*d.* Sheelah Richards *a.* Maurice Davin-Power
The Dreaming Dust	*d.* Michael Barry *a.* Denis Johnston
The Lambs	*d.* Jim Fitzgerald *a.* Criostóir Ó Floinn
An Bullaí	*d.* Brian MacLochlainn *a.* Donncha Ó Ceileachair *adapted by* Seán Ó Tuama
No Trumpets Sounding	*d.* Jim Fitzgerald *a.* Michael Judge
Land *8 episodes*	*d.* Louis Lentin *a.* Liam O'Flaherty *adapted by* Adrian Vale
The Physicists	*d.* Chloe Gibson *a.* Friedrich Durrenmatt
The Far Off Hills	*d.* Sheelah Richards *a.* Lennox Robinson
The Republican Brotherhood *6 episodes*	*d.* Aindreas Ó Gallchoir *a.* Donal McCarthy *adapted by* John O'Donovan
Skipper Next to God	*d.* Gerard Rekers *a.* Jan de Hartog
Happy Days	*d.* Chloe Gibson *a.* Samuel Beckett

Me and My Friend *6 episodes*	*d.* Jim Fitzgerald *a.* Fergus Linehan
Happy as Larry	*d.* Jim Fitzgerald *a.* Donagh MacDonagh
The Fenians	*d.* James Plunkett *a.* Padraic Fallon
Charley's Aunt	*d.* Christopher Fitz-Simon *a.* Brandon Thomas *adapted by* Christopher Fitz-Simon

1968

Tolka Row *serial*	*See page 105.*
The Riordans *serial*	*See page 107.*

A hAon is a hAon sin a hAon
   8 episodes
	d. Donall Farmer
	 a. Eoin Ó Suilleabháin
	     Adrian Vale

How Long is Kissing Time?	*d.* Chloe Gibson *a.* James Douglas
A Cabaret of Savagery and ***Delight***	*d.* Chloe Gibson *a.* Bertolt Brecht
Cradle Song	*d.* Deirdre Friel *a.* Gregorio *and* Mario Martinez Sierra
The Fire Raisers	*d.* Jim Fitzgerald *a.* Max Frisch
The Wild Duck	*d.* Sheelah Richards *a.* Henrik Ibsen
An Giall	*d.* Brian MacLochlainn *a.* Brendan Behan
O'Flaherty V.C.	*d.* Christopher Fitz-Simon *a.* George Bernard Shaw
The Field	*d.* Donall Farmer *a.* John B. Keane

The Testimony of James Connolly	*d.* Eoghan Harris
	a. Eoghan Harris
Killyraggart 17	*d.* Jim Fitzgerald
series	*a.* Fergus Linehan
All the Eels in the Ranny Are Dead	*d.* Sheelah Richards
	a. James Douglas
Defence in Depth	*d.* Chloe Gibson
	a. Patrick Riddel
Flight Into Danger	*d.* Tom McGrath
	a. Arthur Hailey
The Dress Dance	*d.* Jim Fitzgerald
	a. Joe O'Donnell
The Last Eleven	*d.* Michael Barry
	a. Jack White
Pigs in the Parlour	*d.* Jim Fitzgerald
	a. Gilman Noonan
I Have Heard the Mavis Singing	*d.* Peter Kennerley
	a. Michael Judge
Michaelmas Eve	*d.* Christopher Fitz-Simon
	a. T. C. Murray
A Case of Teamwork	*d.* Chloe Gibson
	a. Norman Smythe

1969

The Riordans	*See page 107.*
serial	
Looking at Drama	
5 parts	*d.* Donall Farmer
	Brian MacLochlainn
	Colm Ó Briain
	a. Carolyn Swift
	Laurence Ryan
	Raymond Williams
The Girl from Mayo	*d.* Bill Skinner
	a. Brian Cleeve
	adapted by Carolyn Swift

The Canterville Ghost

d. Christopher Fitz-Simon
a. Oscar Wilde
  adapted by Adrian Vale

The Mother

d. Tony Barry
a. Michael McLaverty
  adapted by Michael Judge

Orpheus and His Lute

d. Brian MacLochlainn
a. Frank O'Connor
  adapted by John McDonnell

Patter O'Rourke

d. Peter Kennerley
a. Walter Macken
  adapted by John Cassidy

Myko

d. Michael Bogdanov
a. Patrick Boyle
  adapted by Wesley Burrowes

Going Into Exile

d. Tony Barry
a. Liam O'Flaherty
  adapted by Eoin Ó Suilleabháin

All the Sweet Buttermilk

d. Michael Bogdanov
a. Donagh MacDonagh
  adapted by Norman Smythe

The Last Troubadour

d. Tom McGrath
a. Donald Giltman

The Deputation

d. Lelia Doolan
a. George A. Bermingham
  adapted by John McDonnell

Guests of the Nation

d. Brian MacLochlainn
a. Frank O'Connor
  adapted by James Douglas

Oilean Tearmainn

d. BrianMacLochlainn
a. Criostoir Ó Floinn

Justice at Large
 8 episodes

d. Tom Kelly
  Jim Fitzgerald
a. Rex Mackey

Southside
 serial

d. Deirdre Friel
a. David Hayes

The Loves of Cass McGuire	*d.* Jim Fitzgerald *a.* Brian Friel
Lady Windermere's Fan	*d.* Chloe Gibson *a.* Oscar Wilde
Antigone	*d.* Sheelah Richards *a.* Jean Anouilh
The Government Inspector	*d.* Donall Farmer *a.* Nikolai Gogol

1970

The Riordans serial	*See page 107.*
King Herod Explains	*d.* Chloe Gibson *a.* Conor Cruise O'Brien
The Gates	*d.* Tony Barry *a.* Jennifer Johnston
A Cruel Fondness	*d.* Chloe Gibson *a.* James Douglas
John Synge Comes Next	*d.* Chloe Gibson *compiled by* Maurice Good
A Change of Management	*d.* Jim Fitzgerald *a.* John Montague *adapted by* Eugene McCabe
The Country Boy	*d.* Donall Farmer *a.* John Murphy *adapted by* Carolyn Swift
The Last Summer	*d.* Jim Fitzgerald *a.* Barbara Walsh
The Prison	*d.* Sheelah Richards *a.* Norman Smythe
Sons and Mothers	*d.* Tony Barry *a.* Wesley Burrowes
The Funeral	*d.* Louis Lentin *a.* Eugene McCabe

Newpark Southside serial	*d.* Laurence Bourne *a.* David Hayes
Over the Bridge	*d.* Chloe Gibson *a.* Sam Thompson
Teacht is Imeacht	*d.* Donall Farmer *a.* Micheál Daltúin
Uncle Vanya	*d.* Louis Lentin *a.* Anton Chekov
The Glorious Uncertainty	*d.* Laurence Bourne *a.* Brinsley McNamara

1971

The Riordans serial	*See page 107.*
What the Butler Missed	*d.* Maurice O'Kelly *a.* Features Dept. team
Saolaiodh Gamhain	*d.* Brian MacLochlainn *a.* Siobhán Ní Suilleabháin
The Rag Pickers	*d.* Chloe Gibson *a.* Norman Smythe
Only the Earth	*d.* Laurence Bourne *a.* Lee Dunne
The Glory and the Dream	*d.* Deirdre Friel *a.* Liam MacUistin
That Rooted Man	*d.* Tony Barry *a.* Denis Johnston
The Becauseway	*d.* Donall Farmer *a.* Wesley Burrowes
The Diary of a Madman	*d.* Donall Farmer *a.* Nikolai Gogol *adapted by* Donall Farmer

---

1972 *Head of Drama 1972–1974: Donall Farmer*

The Riordans serial	*See page 107.*

I Stood Well with All Parties	d. Donall Farmer
	a. Jonah Barrington
I Try to Ignore It, but I Love It	d. Maurice O'Kelly
	a. Fergus Linehan and Neville Fox
An Carabhan	d. Deirdre Friel
	a. Siobhán Ní Shuilleabháin
Who Me?	d. Sheelah Richards
	a. Maureen Donegan
The Lodgers	d. Donall Farmer
	a. Patrick Boyle
What Happens When It Snows?	d. Chloe Gibson
	a. James Douglas
The Lads	d. Sheelah Richards
	a. Joe O'Donnell
A Dog's Life	d. Chloe Gibson
	a. Niall Sheridan
Moloney	d. Brian MacLochlainn
	a. Seán Ó Tuama

1973

The Riordans	See page 107.
serial	
I'm Getting out of This Kip	d. Tony Barry
	a. Heno Magee
The Decoy	d. Brian MacLochlainn
	a. Michael Judge

Portraits
  – The Dean (Jonathan Swift)   d. Chloe Gibson
                                     a. Eugene McCabe

  – The Chief   d. Deirdre Friel
    (Charles Stewart Parnell)   a. Anthony Cronin
  – The Canon (Canon Sheehan)   d. Bill Skinner
                                       a. Eoghan Harris

  – The Rebel (Sean O'Casey)   d. Brian MacLochlainn
                                       a. John Arden
                                             and Margaretta D'Arcy

Famine	*d.* Tony Barry
trilogy	*a.* Tom Murphy
If the Cap Fits	*d.* Brian MacLochlainn
	a. Níall Toibín
	Eoghan Harris
	Wesley Burrowes
	Brendán Ó hEithir
	Brian MacLochlainn
Hair Today, Gone Tomorrow	*d.* Laurence Bourne
	a. Neville Fox
When Handel Played in Dublin	*d.* Chloe Gibson
	a. Wesley Burrowes
Cancer	*d.* Deirdre Friel
	a. Eugene McCabe
Fine Girl You Are	*d.* Sheelah Richards
	a. Anton Chekov
	adapted by Hugh Leonard
	from **The Darling**
Hatchet	*d.* Tony Barry
	a. Heno Magee
Too Short a Summer	*d.* Chloe Gibson
	a. James Douglas

1974

The Riordans	*See page 107.*
serial	
God's Gentry	*d.* Noel O'Briain
	a. Donagh MacDonagh
The Strong Are Lonely	*d.* Chloe Gibson
	a. Fritz Hochwaelder
Exiles	*d.* Donall Farmer
	a. James Joyce
The Promise	*d.* Louis Lentin
	a. Alexei Arbuzov

The Father
    d. Chloe Gibson
    a. August Strindberg

The Rehearsal
    d. Louis Lentin
    a. Jean Anouilh

The House of Bernarda Alba
    d. Sheelah Richards
    a. F. Garcia Lorca

Mother Courage and Her Children
    d. Louis Lentin
    a. Bertolt Brecht

Mr Sing, My Heart's Delight
    d. Brian MacLochlainn
    a. Brian Friel
        adapted by Brian MacLochlainn

The Cuckoo Spit
    d. Deirdre Friel
    a. Mary Lavin

The House That Johnny Built
    d. Tony Barry
    a. Frank O'Connor

A Little Man Dying
    d. Sheelah Richards
    a. Tony Hickey

1975 *Head of Drama 1975–1978: Michael Garvey*

The Riordans
  serial
    See page 107.

Irish Revel
    d. Deirdre Friel
    a. Edna O'Brien

Teangabhail
    d. Brian MacLochlainn
    a. Liam Ó Flatharta

Full Fathom Five
  RTÉ/BBC production
    d. G. P. McCrudden
    a. Michael Judge

The Lads
    d. Laurence Bourne
    a. Joe O'Donnell

Oh, Mistress Mine
    d. Deirdre Friel
    a. Michael Judge

The Flats
    d. Sheelah Richards
    a. John Boyd

Up in the World
  10 episodes
    d. Michael Garvey
    a. David Hayes

The True Story of the Horrid Popish Plot	d. Chloe Gibson a. Desmond Forristal
Voices in the Wilderness	d. Chloe Gibson a. Iris Grant
People in Glass Houses	d. Louis Lentin a. Kevin Grattan
A Cheap Bunch of Nice Flowers	d. Sheelah Richards a. Edna O'Brien
Legion of the Rearguard	d. Noel O'Briain a. Criostoir Ó Floinn

1976

The Riordans serial	*See page 107.*
Nano	d. Desmond Forristal a. Desmond Forristal
Victims trilogy – **Cancer** – – **Heritage** – – **Siege**	d. Deirdre Friel a. EugeneMcCabe
Kilmore House 8 episodes	d. Louis Lentin Chloe Gibson Sheelah Richards Michael Garvey Tony Barry Noel O'Briain a. Norman Smythe James Douglas Conor Farrington Gerry Gallivan Adrian Vale Michael Judge Joe O'Donnell

1977

The Riordans series	*See page 107.*

The Plough and the Stars	*d.* Michael Garvey
	a. Seán O'Casey
Time Now Mr. T.	*d.* Brian MacLochlainn
8 episodes	*a.* Níall Toibín
	Eoghan Harris
	Wesley Burrowes
	Brian MacLochlainn
Eagla	*d.* Michael Garvey
	a. Liam MacUistin
Briarsville Forever	*d.* Louis Lentin
	a. Kevin Grattan
The White House	*d.* Brian MacLochlainn
	a. Tom Murphy
Crystal and Fox	*d.* Noel O'Briain
	a. Brian Friel
King of the Castle	*d.* Louis Lentin
	a. Eugene McCabe

1978 *Head of Drama 1978–1980: Louis Lentin*

The Riordans	*See page 107.*
series	
The Spike	*d.* Noel O'Briain
10 episodes - withdrawn after	Brian MacLochlainn
5th episode	*a.* Patrick Gilligan
Teems of Times	*d.* Louis Lentin
10 episodes	*a.* Dominic Behan
The Last of Summer	*d.* Donall Farmer
4 parts	*a.* Kate O'Brien
	adapted by Tony Hickey
The Tailor and Ansty	*d.* Laurence Bourne
	a. Eric Cross
	adapted by Laurence Bourne
The Heart's a Wonder	*d.* Laurence Bourne
	a. John Millington Synge
	adapted by Maureen *and*

	Nuala O'Farrell *from* **The Playboy of the Western World**
The Burke Enigma	d. Brian MacLochlainn a. Michael Feeney Callan
Deeply Regretted by …	d. Louis Lentin a. Maeve Binchy

1979

The Riordans serial	*See page 107.*
Silver Apples on the Moon	d. John Lynch a. Wesley Burrowes
Farmers	d. Michael Garvey a. Thomas Kilroy
Mobile Homes	d. Pat O'Connor a. Jim Sheridan
God's in His Heaven	d. Michael Garvey a. Michael Judge
Langrishe, Go Down RTÉ/BBC co-production	d. David Jones a. Aidan Higgins *adapted by* Harold Pinter
The Apprentice	d. Seán Cotter a. Eugene McCabe
The Sash	d. Donall Farmer a. Hector McMillan
Roma	d. Louis Lentin a. Eugene McCabe
Inquiry at Knock	d. Seán Cotter a. Desmond Forristal
Miracles and Miss Langan	d. Pat O'Connor a. Neil Jordan
Whose Child?	d. Deirdre Friel a. Michael Judge

Passing Through	*d.* Peter Farrell
	a. Alun Owen
Gale Day	*d.* Pat O'Connor
	a. Eugene McCabe
If You're Irish	*d.* Peter Farrell
	a. Ron Hutchinson
On the Feast of Stephen	*d.* Deirdre Friel *and* Pat O'Connor
	a. Wesley Burrowes

1980 *Head of Drama 1980–1982: Tony Barry*

Assault on a Citadel	*d.* Noel O'Briain
	a. Sean Walsh
Bracken	*d.* Noel O'Briain
6 *episodes*	*a.* Wesley Burrowes
An Taoille Tuile	*d.* Donall Farmer
	a. Mairtín Ó Cadhain
Scruples	*d.* Peter Ormrod
	a. Tom MacIntyre
Teresa's Wedding	*d.* Donall Farmer
	a. William Trevor
Visitors	*d.* Peter Ormrod
	a. Edmund Ward
The Babysitters	*d.* Pat O'Connor
	a. Peter Driscoll
Strumpet City	*d.* Tony Barry
7 *episodes*	*a.* James Plunkett
	adapted by Hugh Leonard
The Silver Tassie	*d.* Brian MacLochlainn
	a. Seán O'Casey
Ireland of the Welcomes	*d.* Deirdre Friel
	a. Maeve Binchy
One for Sorrow	*d.* Peter Ormrod
not transmitted	*a.* Sean McCarthy
If You Want to Know Me	*d.* Seán Cotter
	a. David Hayes

| *Payoff* | *d.* Peter Ormrod |
| | *a.* Kevin Grattan |

| *Your Favourite Funnyman* | *d.* Michael O'Connell |
| | *a.* Martin Duffy |

| *Airc* | *d.* Noel O'Briain |
| | *a.* Gabriel Rosenstock |

Sean	*d.* Louis Lentin
13 episodes	*a.* Michael Voysey
	Neil Jordan
	Eugene McCabe

1981

The Ante Room	*d.* Seán Cotter
4 parts	*a.* Kate O'Brien
	adapted by Tony Hickey

| *The Parting Gift* | *d.* Seán Cotter |
| | *a.* Barbara McKeon |

| *The Bondage Field* | *d.* John Lynch |
| | *a.* Jennifer Johnston |

| *Winter Music* | *d.* Pat O'Connor |
| | *a.* Eugene McCabe |

| *The Second Last Post* | *d.* Tony Barry |
| | *a.* Lee Gallaher |

| *Love is …* | *d.* John McColgan |
| | *a.* Michael Callan |

| *Men of Consequence* | *d.* Barry Kelly |
| | *a.* Martin Duffy |

| *Amy* | *d.* Paul Cusack |
| | *a.* Barbara McKeon |

| *Legs Eleven* | *d.* Bill Keating |
| *not transmitted* | *a.* Bernard Farrell |

1982 *Head of Drama 1982–1986: Niall McCarthy*

| *The Dreamers* | *d.* Paul Cusack |
| | *a.* Seán Walsh |

Bracken 2
  6 episodes

d. Noel O'Briain
a. Wesley Burrowes

The Lost Hour

d. Seán Cotter
a. John McGahern
  adapted by Carlo Gebler *from*
  The Leavetaking

Choosing

d. Seán Cotter
a. Maureen Donegan

The Ballroom of Romance
  RTÉ/BBC co-production

d. Pat O'Connor
a. William Trevor

The Year of the French
  6 episodes
  RTÉ/Channel 4/FR3 co-production

d. Michael Garvey
a. Thomas Flanagan
  adapted by Eugene McCabe

1983

The Irish RM
  serial
  RTÉ/Channel 4 co-production

d. Robert Chetwyn
a. Somerville and Ross
  adapted by Rosemary Ann Sissons

Roses from Dublin
  6 episodes
  RTÉ/Technisionar co-production

d. Lazare Iglesias
p. Paul Cusack
a. Pierre Rey

One of Ourselves
  RTÉ/BBC co-production

d. Pat O'Connor
a. William Trevor

Glenroe
  serial
n.b. The listing of producers,
directors and authors relates to
the entire run of the programme
up to 1987.

d. Brian MacLochlainn
  Noel O'Briain
  Avril McRory
  Deirdre Friel
  Laurence Bourne
  John Lynch
  Anne McCabe
  Claire O'Loughlin
a. Wesley Burrowes
  Lee Gallaher
  Dennis Lattimer
  Biddy White-Lennon

Caught in a Free State
  4 parts
  RTÉ/Channel 4 co-production

d. Peter Ormrod
a. Brian Lynch

Night in Tunisia
   RTÉ/Channel 4 co-production

   d. Pat O'Connor
   a. Neil Jordan

Good Behaviour
   3 parts
   RTÉ/BBC co-production

   d. Bill Hays
   a. Molly Keane
      adapted by Hugh Leonard

The Key

   d. Tony Barry
   a. John McGahern
      adapted by Carlo Gebler

Still Love

   d. Noel O'Briain
   a. Barbara McKeon

1984

Glenroe
   serial

See page 125.

Painted Out

   d. Louis Lentin
   a. Tom MacIntyre

Tales of Kilnavarna
   6 episodes

   d. Bill Keating
   a. John B. Keane
      adapted by Joe O'Donnell

Love Stories of Ireland
   RTÉ/Channel 4 co-production
   – Lovers of the Lake

   p. John Lynch

   d. Tony Barry
   a. Sean O Faolain
      adapted by Alun Owen

   – Access to the Children

   d. Tony Barry
   a. William Trevor

   – The Eagles and the Trumpets

   d. Deirdre Friel
   a. James Plunkett

   – A Painful Case

   d. John Lynch
   a. James Joyce
      adapted by Michael Voysey

Leave It to Mrs. O'Brien
   13 episodes

   d. Brian MacLochlainn
   a. Angela McFadden
      Joe Dunlop

1985

Glenroe
   serial

See page *125.*

The Price
  6 episodes
  RTÉ/Channel 4 co-production

p. Mark Shivas
d. Peter Smith
a. Peter Ransley

Raic

d. Noel Ó Briain
a. Antoine Ó Flatharta

A Life

d. Louis Lentin
a. Hugh Leonard

Summer Lightning

p. Michael Garvey
d. Paul Joyce
a. Ivan Turgenev
  adapted by Paul Joyce *and* Derek
  Mahon *from* **First Love**

Spring Cleaning

d. Tony Barry
a. Ann Barrett

Inside
  serial

d. Noel Ó Briain
  Gerry Stembridge
a. Joe Dunlop
  Mannix Flynn
  Lee Dunne
  Noel Ó Briain

Stowaway
  RTÉ/EBU production

d. Joe O'Donnell
a. Joe O'Donnell

1986 *Head of Drama since 1986: Noel Ó Briain*

Glenroe
  serial

See page 125.

Leave it to Mrs O'Brien
  series

See page 126.

Access Community Drama
  – **Fresh Salmon**
  – **The Changeling**
  – **Win Some, Lose Some**
  – **There Has to be a Reason**
  – **Emigrants**
  – **Moving On**
  – **Vandals**

Olivian Players, Dublin
Relays Productions, Ballinasloe
Rush Dramatic Society
Leixlip Theatre Group
Charlestown Little Theatre Group
The Moat Club, Naas
Everyman Productions, Sligo

The Island
                                       d. Louis Lentin
                                       a. Athol Fugard
                                            John Kani
                                            Winston Ntshona

Partners in Practice
   serial
                  d. Laurence Bourne
                  a. Carolyn Swift
                        James Douglas
                        Michael Judge

The Seamen
          d. Chloe Gibson
          a. Norman Smythe

The Treaty Debates
          d. Donall Farmer
          a. G. P. Gallivan and Kevin B. Nowlan

Mr. Joyce Is Leaving Paris
          d. Louis Lentin
          a. Tom Gallagher

The Emigrant
          d. Tony Barry
          a. Paddy Fahy

The Branchy Tree
          d. Chloe Gibson
          a. extracts from Irish literature

Andorra
          d. Louis Lentin
          a. Max Frisch
              adapted by Adrian Vale

A Week in the Life of Martin Cluxton
          d. Brian MacLochlainn
          a. Caoimhín Ó Marcaigh and
              Brian MacLochlainn

Riders to the Sea
          d. Sheelah Richards
          a. John Millington Synge

RTÉ/Irish television drama productions, 1987–2002

Compiled by Carole Jones

1987

Glenroe *serial n. b. The listing of directors and authors relates to the entire run of the programme 1987–2002.*

d. Anne McCabe, Claire O'Loughlin, Brian MacLochlainn, Seán Cotter, Tom McArdle, John Lynch, Noel Ó Briain, Joe O'Donnell, Art Ó Briain, Charlie McCarthy, Antoine Ó Flatharta, Deirdre Friel, Michael Heney, David McKenna, Alan Robinson

a. Wesley Burrowes, Bernard Farrell, Dennis Latirner, Biddy White Lennon, Bryan Lynch, Patrick Gilligan, Michael Judge, Harriet O'CarrolL Lee Gallaher, Maeve Ingoldsby, Joe O'Donnell, Sean McCarthy, Ellis Ní Dhuibhne, John McArdle, Andy Black, Jennifer O'Hara, Michael Cussen, Jack Ward

Leave It to Mrs O'Brien	d. Brian MacLachlainn
3rd series 12 episodes	a. Joe Dunlop
Where Reason Sleeps	
RTÉ/Strongbow/Channel 4 co-production	
– Fear of the Dark	d. Tony Barry
	a. Robert Wynne-Simmons
– Out of Time	d. Robert Wynne-Simmons
	a. Ronald Frame
– A Summer Ghost	d. Robert Wynne Simmons
– The Scar	d. Robert Wynne-Simmons
Nothing to It	a. & d. Gerard Stembridge

Clash of the Ash
  Circus Films/RTÉ/BSE/Comhairle
  Éalaion co-production

a. & d. Fergus Tighe

A Cow in the Water

d. & a. Nicholas Pole
from a Polly Devlin *story*

Stories from Ireland
  Eamon Kelly stories

p. & d. Niall McCarthy

1988

Glenroe

See page 129.

Brigit

d. Noel O Briain
a. Tom Murphy

Lotty Coyle Loves Buddy Holly

d. Tony Barry
a. Bernard Farrell

Errors and Omissions

d. John Lynch
a. Lee Gallaher

The Black Knight

p. & d. Gerard Stembridge
a. Brian Mitchell

Drama Seven – Stowaway
  RTÉ's contribution to a series of
  dramas for young people

Series Producer Joe O'Donnell

Echoes
  4 episodes
  Working Title production for RTÉ
  and Channel 4

d. & a. Barbara Rennie
adaptation of a Maeve Binchy
novel

Act of Betrayal
  2 episodes
  Griffen/RTE/TVS/
  Australian Broadcasting
  Corporation co-production

d. Lawrence Gordon Clark

a. Nick Evans & Michael Chaplin

Commonplaces
  5 episodes

d. & a. Gerard Stembridge

Shades of the Jelly Woman

d. Christopher Fitz-Simon
a. Peter Sheridan
  in collaboration with Jean Doyle

Decó
  Total Video Production for RTÉ

d. Paddy McClintock
a. Gabriel Rosenstock

Nighthawks
  topical satire series

An Independent Eye
  series of new drama on film:
  – **Budawanny**
    Cinegael Channel 4
  – **Lapsed Catholics**
    Windmill Lane/RTÉ co-production
  – **Boom Babies**
    Amantango Productions/BSÉ/RTÉ
  – **Frankie and Johnny**
    Dún Laoghaire Institute of Art,
    Design and Technology
  – **Goodbye Piccadilly**
    Dún Laoghaire Institute of Art,
    Design and Technology

d. & a. Bob Quinn
from the novel by Pádraig Standúin
d. & a. Barry Devlin

d. &a. Siobhán Twomey

d. & a. Liam O'Neill

d. & p. Kieran J. Walsh

1989

Glenroe
See page 129.

Fair City
serial n. b. The listing of directors and authors relates to entire run of the programme

d. Chris Clough, Seán Cotter, Philip Draycott, David McKenna, Fiona Cumming, Mike Gibbon, Paul Cusack, John Lynch, Malcolm Taylor, Nicholas Prosser, John. Williams, Ron Francis, Sheila Atha, William Slater, Garth Tucker, Bill Keating, Deirdre Friel, John Comisky, Niall Matthews, Declan Eames, Patrick Tucker, Henry Foster, Geoff Husson, Una Pierce, Paul Fitzgerald, Gary Agnew, John McHugh, Phil Hill, Marion Creely, Stephen Butcher, Brian Morgan, Vivienne Cozens, Charlie McCarthy, Neasa Hardiman, Chris Johnston, Fiona Keane, Jonathan Wright Miller, Oliver Horsbrugh, Trevor Ó Clochartaigh, Anita Notaro.

a. Peter Sheridan, Brian Byrne, Harriet O'Carroll, Maeve Ingoldsby, Margaret Neylon, Pearse McCaughey, Ned Tobin, Lee Dunne, Rio Fanning, Ena May, Laurence Byrne, Sean Moffatt, Lauren MacKenzie, Mary Halpin, Catherine Brophy, Marie Hannigan, Linsey Sedgewick, Niall McGarrigle, Seamus Moran, Thomas McLaughlin, Michael Cussen, Frances Kay, Clive Geraghty,

Joni Crone, Frank Gannon, Ted Gannon, Fiona Daly, Paul Walker, Bill Tierney, Carmel Callan, Kevin McGee, Liz Bono, Barbara McKeon, Clare Dowling, Brian Gallagher, Robert Taylor, Bernie Downes, Barbara Parkinson, Sian Quill, Pat Maher, Anthony O'Keefe, Hilary Reynolds, Collette Cullen, Dympna Clarke, Mark Wale, Gerald Murphy, John Fagan, Siobhan Miley.

All about Alfie
  drama documentary   *p. & a.* Art Ó Bríain

Nighthawks
  topical satire series

Molloy
  6-part comedy series   *p. & d.* Tom McArdle
                                         a. Paul O'Loughlin

Samuel Beckett – Three Plays: *d.* Walter D. Asmus

  Eh Joe, Footfalls, Rockabye
  RM Associates/Suddeutscher Rundfunk/
  Channel 4/RTÉ co-production

My Left Foot   *d.* Jim Sheridan
  RTÉ/Ferndale Films/   *a.* Shane Connaughton
  Granada Television International   & Jim Sheridan
  co-production   *based on the book by* Christy Brown

Nights of Revolution   *a. & d.* Charles Brabant
  RTÉ/RM Arts/La Sept/FR3/   *adapted from the writings of*
  Philippe Dussart co-production   Nicolas Restif de la Bretonne

The Mahabharata
  3 episodes   *d.* Peter Brook
  RTÉ/Brooklyn Academy of Music/
  Les Productions Deuxième Etage
  co-production

The Real Charlotte   *d.* Tony Barry
  Gandon Productions   *a.* Bernard MacLaverty
                                         adaptation of the novel by
                                         Somerville and Ross

1990

Glenroe   *See page 129.*

Fair City   *See page 131–2.*

Deco
   Total Video production for RTÉ

                                              p. & d. Paddy McClintock

Nighthawks
   topical satire series

Dear Sarah
                                             d. Frank Cvitanovich
                                           a. Tom McGurk

Fragments of Isabella
                                           d. Ronan O'Leary
                                           a. Gabrielle Reidy & Michael Scott
                                             adapted from the book by Isabella Leitner

By the Roadside: Vincent Van Gogh and the Others
   4 episodes
   RTÉ/NOS/BRT/RMR Arts co-production
                                           d. Jan Keja

The Confessions of Blaithin Keaveney   *Series producer* David Blake-Knox

Hush-A-Bye Baby
   Derry Film and Video Workshop/ Channel 4/British Screen Finance/RTÉ/ Arts Council of Ireland co-production
                                           d. Margo Harkin
                                           a. Margo Harkin & Stephanie English

Mise Agus Pangur Bán
                                           d. Gerard Stembridge
                                           p. Máire Ní Thúthail

Grásta I mEiriceá
   Deilt/RTÉ co-production
                                           d. Noel O'Briain
                                           a. Antoine Ó Flatharta

The Lilac Bus
   Little Bird Vision for RTÉ
                                           d. Giles Foster
                                         a. Shane Connaughton
                                             adapted from novel by Maeve Binchy

First View
   series of new drama on film:
   – **London Calling**   *d. & a.* Peter Mulryan
   – **Suspicious Mind**   *p.* Hugh Farley
   – **That's All Right**   *p.* Billy McCannon
   – **Big Swinger**   *d. & a.* Declan Recks
      Dún Laoghaire Institute of Art, Design and Technology Paradox Pictures

– *Jack's Bicycle*   *d. & a.* John Moore
– *Undercurrents*   *d. & a.* Stephen Rooke
  Tile Films Ltd for RTÉ
– *No Flowers*   *d.* Alan Archbold
  Echo Productions/Early Town Films   *a.* Patrick O'Donoghue
– *Awakening*   *d.* Don McLave & Michael
                                    Dunne Jnr

– *End of Part Three*   *d. & a.* Iain Keeney
  Dún Laoghaire Institute of Art,
  Design and Technology/Tuna Fish
  Productions

1991

Glenroe   *See page 129.*

Fair City   *See page 131.*

Hard Shoulder   *d. & a.* Mark Kilroy
  Mirror Film for RTÉ and Channel 4

The Truth about Claire   *p. and d.* Gerard Stembridge

Nighthawks
  topical satire series

Events at Drimaghleen   *d.* Robert Cooper
  RTÉ/BBCNI co-production   *a.* William Trevor

Brides of Christ
  6 episodes   *d.* Ken Cameron
  ABC TC/Roadshow/Coote &Carroll/   *a.* John Alsop
  Channel 4/RTÉ co-production

Eh Joe   *d.* Alan Gilsenan
  RTÉ/Yellow Asylum Films   *a.* Samuel Beckett *original screenplay*
  with assistance from BSÉ

Bossanova Blues   *d. & a.* Kieron J. Walsh
  RTÉ/Royal College of Art co-production

Jabas
  Telegael production for RTÉ

The Treaty   *d.* Jonathan Lewis
  Merlin Films for RTÉ and Thames
  Television   *a.* Brian Phelan

Diary of a Madman

p. & d. Ronan O'Leary
a. Tim O'Donnell *adapted from the story* by Nikolai Gogol

First View
series of new drama on film:
– **Splice of Life**   *d. & a.* Martin Duffy
– **One Day Return**   *d. & a.* Jim Newport
  Dún Langhaire Institute of Art, Design and Technology
– **Stephen**   *d. & a.* Johnny Gogan
  Bandit Films (Grand Pictures)/ Film Base/RTÉ
– **The Long Wake**   *d. & a.* Kieran Concannon
– **Young at Heart**   *d. & a.* Susan Brennan
  Dún Langhaire Institute of Art, Design and Technology
– **Murmurs**   *d. & a.* Bryan Meade
  College of Commerce Rathmines
– **Shelley and the Doctor**   *d.* Kelly Ann O'Neill
– **Heartline**   *d. & a.* Julian Plunkett Dillon

1992

Fair City   *See page 129.*

Glenroe   *See page 131.*

Jabas
  Telegael production for RTÉ

Conneely's Choice   *d.* Barra de Bhaldraithe
  Scannain Beal/RTÉ co-production   *an adaptation of Scottish/Irish seal legends of the Atlantic*

Ros na Rún
Irish language drama serial   *d.* Deirdre Friel
Léiriú le Telebo ar son RTÉ agus   *p.* Con Bushe
Udarás na Gaeltachta co-production   *a.* Antoine Ó Flatharta

Nighthawks
  topical satire series

The Treaty   *d. & p.* Jonathan Lewis
  RTÉ/Thames Television co-production   *a.* Brian Phelan

Force of Duty
  BBCNI/RTÉ co-production

d. Pat O'Connor
a. Bill Morrison & Chris Ryder

1993

Ros na Rún
  serial

See page 135.

Glenroe
  serial

See page 129.

Fair City
  serial

See pages 131–2.

The Bargain Shop
  Bandit Films/RTÉ/
  ZDF TV co-production

d. & a. Johnny Gogan

Tá an Saol ina Dhiabhal
  6 episodes drama series for teenagers
  Telegael a rinne an leagan Gaeilge do/RTÉ

Henri
  BBCNI/RTÉ co-production

d. Simon Shore
a. John Forte

Horse
  Picture House Productions/Film Base/
  RTÉ co-production

d. & a. Kevin Liddy

Extra! Extra! Read All About It
  series 8 episodes

d. Alastair Clark
a. Frank Sheerin

High Boot Benny
  Sandy/RTE/ZDS co-production
  in association with BSÉ, Channel 4,
  Greco, TVC and La Sept

d. Joe Comerford

Korea
  RTÉ/ZDF/BSÉ

d. Cathal Black
a. Joe O'Byrne *from a short story* by
  John McGahern

Circle of Friends
  Price Entertainment/Lantana
  Productions/Savoy Pictures

d. Pat O'Connor
a. Andrew Davies *from the novel by*
  Maeve Binchy

First View
  series of new drama on film:
  – **Noctave**   *d. & a.* Siochfiadha Kelly
    Dún Laughaire Institute of Art,
    Design and Technology
  – **Heaven Only Knows**   *d.* Liam Regan
    Dún Laughaire Institute of Art,
    Design and Technology
  – **Booth**   *d.* Petra Conroy
    Dublin Institute of Technology
  – **There's a Hole in the Ozone Layer**
    just above Clonbroo   *d. & a.* Bill McCannon
    Little Bird
  – **The Barber Shop**   *d. & a.* Liam O'Neill
    Paradox Pictures /Mainstream Films
  – **Matrix Adjusted**   *d. & p.* Conor O'Mahony
  – **Mind's Eye**   *d. a. p.* Paul Giles
    Dún Laughaire Institute of Art,
    Design and Technology
  – **Whippets**   *d.* Greg du Fay
    Dublin Institute of Technology
  – **Blind Alley**   *d.* Paul Duane
    Blind Alley Productions KFR Inc.
    BBC Bristol
  – **Two Wasters**   *d. & a.* Owen McPolin
    Owen McPolin Productions
  – **Bound for Manhattan**   *d. & a.* Ciaran Donnelly
    Dún Laughaire Institute of Art,
    Design and Technology
  – **The Dadson Rites**   *d. & a.* Garry Keane
    Dún Laughaire Institute of Art,
    Design and Technology
  – **The Last Word**   *d. & a.* Lee Rooney
    Dún Laughaire Institute of Art, Design
    and Technology, Galway Corporation
  – **Corkscrew**   *d. & a.* Ben Yeates
    Dún Laughaire Institute of Art,
    Design and Technology
  – **A Stone of the Heart**   *d.* Paddy Breathnach
    Treasure Films   *a.* Joseph O'Connor
  – **One Man One Woman**   *d.* Joe Tanham

– *Atonement*   *d. & a.* James Finlan
Galway Film Centre/
Hysterie Film Productions

– *Icarus*   *d. & a.* Jonathan White
Dún Laughaire Institute of Art,
Design and Technology

– *The Visit*   *d. & a.* Orla Walsh
Grand Pictures/Film Bas/
Dublin Institute of Technology

– *Love Is a Very Fickle Thing*   *d. & a.* Mark Staunton
Dogtown Productions

– *The Sea*   *d.* Richard West
– *Exit*   *d.* Suzanne O'Toole
– *Lily's Christmas* (*no production credits*)
– *Into the Abyss*   *d. & a.* Geraldine Creed
Blue Light Productions

– *Messenger Boy*   *d.* Mick Foran
– *Crossed Lines*   *d. & a.* Neal Boyle
Dún Laughaire Institute of Art,
Design and Technology

– *About War*   *d.* Miguel Alexandre
– *Octopusses Don't Fly*   *d.* Norbert Payne
– *The Family*   *d. & p.* Bob Quin
– *To Forget*   *d.* David Quin

1994

Glenroe   *See page 129.*

Fair City   *See pages 131–2.*

All Things Bright and Beautiful   Barry Devlin
Hilltown/Good Film/
BBCNI/RTÉ co-production

Family
4 episodes   *d.* Mike Winterbottom
RTÉ/BBC co-production   *a.* Roddy Doyle

Two Lives
series of plays for television   *Series producer* Michael Colgan
                                   Executive producer David Blake-Knox

– *A Mother's Love Is a Blessing*   *d.* Charlie McCarthy
                                   a. Pat McCabe

– Seachange　　　　　　　　　　*d.* Thaddeus O'Sullivan
　　　　　　　　　　　　　　　　a. John Banville

– Boston Rose　　　　　　　　　　*d.* Ferdia MacAnna
　　　　　　　　　　　　　　　　a. Antoine Ó Flatharta

– The Celadon Cup　　　　　　　*d.* Deirdre Friel
　　　　　　　　　　　　　　　　a. Hugh Leonard

– Black and White　　　　　　　　*d.* Alan Robinson
　　　　　　　　　　　　　　　　a. Kathy Gilfillan

– Revenge　　　　　　　　　　　　*d.* Dearbhla Walsh
　　　　　　　　　　　　　　　　a. Anne Enright

– Tossed Salad　　　　　　　　　*d.* Anne McCabe
　　　　　　　　　　　　　　　　a. Catherine Donnelly

– In High Germany　　　　　　　*d.* Brian MacLochlainn
　　　　　　　　　　　　　　　　a. Dermot Bolger

– Gold in the Streets　　　　　　*d.* Thaddeus O'Sullivan
　　　　　　　　　　　　　　　　a. Thomas Kilroy

The Barber Shop　　　　　　　　*d. & a.* Liam O'Neill
　Film Base/RTÉ co-production

Thou Shalt Not Kill
　drama documentary series:
　– The Green Tureen　　　　　　*d.* Dearbhla Walsh
　　　　　　　　　　　　　　　　a. Ingrid Craigie

　– The Kerry Killings　　　　　　*d.* Paul Cusack
　　　　　　　　　　　　　　　　a. Kevin O'Connor

　– My Aunt in Drumcondra　　　*d.* Deirdre Friel
　　　　　　　　　　　　　　　　a. Kevin O'Connor

　– The Car in Corbawn Lane　　*d.* Alan Robinson
　　　　　　　　　　　　　　　　a. Cathal O'Shannon

　– The Mystery of Ireland 's Eye　*d.* Paul Cusack
　　　　　　　　　　　　　　　　a. Fiona Daly

Ailsa　　　　　　　　　　　　　*d.* Paddy Breathnach
　Emperor Films in Ireland/　　　*a.* Joseph O'Connor
　Temple Film and Television/
　WDR/RTÉ/ARTE co-production

Misteach Baile Atha Cliath　　*d.* Paul Duane
　Ciotóg Films/RTÉ co-production　*a.* Seamus McAnnadaith

A Christmas Snap　　　　　　　*d. & a.* Brian O'Flaherty

First View
  series of new drama on film:
  – **God Suit**   *d. & a.* Fionn Seavers
    Dún Laoghaire Institute of Art,
    Design and Technology
  – **The Pigeon Lady**   *d. & a.* Aidan Mckeown
    Dublin Institute of Technology
  – **Priesthunter**   *d. & a.* Michael Brennan
    Sundance Films/Galway Film Resource
  – **Boys for Rent**   *d. & a.* Liam McGrath
    Dún Laoghaire Institute of Art,
    Design and Technology
  – **Berlin Blues**   *d. & a.* Kathleen O'Driscoll
  – **Arkansas**   *d. & a.* Gary Clarke
    Shrinking Man Productions
  – **The Book of Ghosts**   *d.* David Bickley
    Rare Earth/Telegael   *a.* Michael Comyns
  – *A Student Film*   *d. & a.* Alan Duffy
    Dublin Institiute of Technology
  – *Changelings*   *d. & a.* Dee Armstrong
    Dún Laoghaire Institute of Art,
    Design and Technology
  – *Fruit 15*   *d. & a.* Claire Lynch
    Dún Laoghaire Institute of Art,
    Design and Technology
  – **No Better Man**   *d.* Caitriona Ryan
    Black Puddin' Productions   *a.* Christine Dwyer Hickey
  – Principles of Physics   *d. & a.* Ellen J. Kavanagh
    Angels on the Head of a Pin
    Productions/Galway Film Centre
  – **Wasted**   *d. & a.* Michael McAuley
  – **The Clock**   *d.* Patrick Hodgins
    Dublin Institute of Technology   *a.* Teresa Hogan
  – **War**   *d. & a.* Gerard Maycock
    Dún Laoghaire Institute of Art,
    Design and Technology

1995

Glenroe   See page 129.
  series

Fair City   *See pages 131–2.*
  series

Seanchaí
*Irish language series of dramatised tales of the supernatural. A Northlands production
for RTÉ*
  Series Editor Nuala Ní Dhomhnaill
  – *An Póitsealaí agus an Maor Uisce*
   (The Poacher and the Bailiff)
  – *An t-Adhlacóir*
   (The Undertaker)
  – *An Sceach*
   (The Thorn Tree)
  – *An Sealag Campáil*
   (The Camping Holiday)
  – *Altdir na Bealtaine*
   (The May Altar)
  – *An Tobar Fioruisce*
   (The Well)

A House in Jerusalem
  series, dramatisation of the life and   *d.* Dearbhla Walsh
  sayings of Jesus Christ   *a.* Suzanne Heine & Joe O'Donnell
  RTÉ Religious Programmes/
  ORF co-production

The Hanging Gale
  4-part serial   *d.* Diarmuid Lawrence
  Little Bird/RTÉ/BBCNI/   *a.* Allan Cubitt
  BSE co-production

The Stranger within Me   *d.* Geraldine Creed
  Blue Light Productions/Film Base/
  RTÉ co-production

Stephen   *d. & a.* Johnny Gogan
  Bandit Films/Film Base/
  RTÉ co-production

Upwardly Mobile
  series n. b. The list of writers and directors relates to entire run of the programme.
  d. Tom Poole, Pennant Roberts, Jeff Naylor.
  a. Ted Gannon, Thomas McLaughlin, Bill Tierney, James Corry, Moya Roddy,
Brian Lynch, Joe O'Donnell, Kevin McGee, Stephen Walsh, Louise Geraghty,

David D Wilson, Brigitte Downey, Eamonn Kelly, Michael Jordan, Jim Eldridge, the Vopins, Kevin Lynch, Alan Pollack, Rachel Moriarty, Peter Murphy, Tom Denver.

Finbar's Class
series   *d. & p.* Roy Heayberd
a. Michael Sheridan &
Jennifer O'Hara

Thou Shalt Not Kill
drama documentary series:
  – **Murder in the Park**   *d.* Paul Cusack
a. Cathal O'Shannon

  – **Summer Lemonade**   *d.* Gary Agnew
a. Fiona Daly

  – **Mystery at Marlhill**   *d.* Philip McGovern
a. Kevin O'Connor

  – **A Desperate Affair**   *d.* Alan Robinson
a. Kate Kavanagh

  – **Sanctuary**   *d.* Michael Heney
a. Kevin O'Connor

  – **The True Story of the Colleen Bawn** *d.* Ferdia MacAnna
a. Kevin Grattan

Guiltrip   *d. & a.* Gerard Stembridge
Temple Films/Fandango Smile Productions

First View
series of new drama on film:
  – **Skin Tight**   *d. & a.* John Forte
First City Features Productions/
Northern Lights
  – **Change**   *d.* Ger Philpot
  – **Sunny's Deliverance**   *p.* Declan Recks
Paradox Pictures
  – **After 68**   *d.* Stephen Burke
Mammoth Films/Dublin Institute of
Technology/Cornerstone Pictures
  – **The Connivers**   *d.* David Caffrey
  – **The Barrel**   *d. & a.* Michael O'Donovan
Dún Laoghaire Institute of Art,
Design and Technology/
Stone Ridge Entertainment

– *The Life of Reilly*   *d. & a.* Alan Archbold
  Early Town Films
– *Darkest Hours*   *d. p. & a.* Conan McCabe
– *Business as Usual*   *d.* Matt Rodgers
  Creggan Films
– *Where the Heart Remains*   *d.* Alison Twomey
– *Blinder*   *d. & a.* Eve Morrison
  Dún Laoghaire Institute of Art,
  Design and Technology/Camel Productions

RTÉ Independent Productions Unit
commissioned drama:
– *All Souls Day*   *d. & a.* Alan Gilsenan
  Yellow Asylum Films
– *The Disappearance of Finbar*   *d.* Sue Clayton
  Samson Films   *a.* Dermot Bolger & Sue Clayton
– *Joe My Friend*   *d.* Chris Bould
  Promedia   *a.* David Howard & Declan Hughes
– *Boys and Men*   *d.* Sean Hinds
  Parallel Films   *a.* Brian Lally
– *Poorhouse*   *d.* Frank Stapleton
  Ocean Films   *a.* Frank Stapleton & Michael Harding
– *The Sun, the Moon and the Stars*   *d. & a.* Geraldine Creed
  Blue Light Productions
– *The Boy from Mercury*   *d. & a.* Martin Duffy
  Mercurian Productions

1996

Glenroe   *See page 129.*
  serial

Fair City   *See pages 131–2.*
  serial

A House in Jerusalem   *d. & d.* Dearbhla Walsh
  RTÉ Religious Programmes/   *executive producer* Dermod McCarthy
  ORF co-production

Sara   *d. & p.* Robin Crichton
       executive producer Kevin Linehan

Scene
  teenage drama series
  BBC/RTÉ co-production:
  – ***Edward No Hands***   d. Charles McCarthy
                                          a. Dermot Bolger

  – ***Radio Waves***   d. & p. Anne McCabe
                                            a. Bernard Farrell

  – ***Terraces***   d. Rob Rohrer
                                            a. Willy Russell

  – ***SAB***   d. Edwina Vardey
                                            a. Michael Cook

  – ***Thin Ice***   d. Nicci Crowther
                                          a. Grazyna Monvid

  – ***Teaching Matthew***   d. Sharon Miller
                                          a. Al Hunter Ashton

  – ***Pig Boy***   d. Simon Cellan Jones
                                          a. Stephen Handley

  – ***Dear Life***   d. Jane Howell
                                          a. Sue Glover

  – ***Pride***   d. Edwina Vardey
                                          a. Peter Barnes

  – ***The Soldier***   d. Jean Stewart
                                          a. Sarah Holmes

  – ***Young Jung***   d. Juliet May
                                          a. Howard Schuman

  – ***Career Opportunities***   d. John Lynch

Dear Daughter
  drama documentary   d. & p. Louis Lentin
  Crescendo Concept/Sablegrange Ltd/
  RTÉ/BSÉ co-production

Upwardly Mobile   *See page 141.*
  series

Finbar's Class   *See page 142.*
  series

Ros na Rún
Irish language serial
produced by Eo Teilefís/Tír Eoghain from original idea by Con Bushe of RTÉ
d. Deirdre Friel, Art Ó Briain, Charlie McCarthy, Trevor Ó Clochartaigh, Claire O'Loughlin, Malcolm Ó Táilliúir, Stephen Butcher, Brian Morgan, Derbhla Walsh, Traolach Ó Buachalla, Clare Wilde, Deirdre Ní Flatharta, Sue Dunderdale, Hugh Farley.
a. Antoine Ó Flatharta, Greg O'Braonáin, Ailbhe Nic Giolla Bhríghde, Anne Learmont, Padraigh Ó Giollagain.

CU Burn   d. Niall Mac Eachmharcaigh
Lios na Sifor TnaG

Gleann Ceo
Irish language comedy drama serial   p. Seán Mac Fhionnghaile
Cúl A Tigh for TnaG

Trojan Eddie   d. Gillies MacKinnon, Andrew
Stratford Productions/TroVan Eddie   Hegarty, Suzanne Nicell
Productions/Irish Screen   a. Billy Roche

November Afternoon   d. & a. John Carney & Tom Hall
High Hat Productions/Early Town Films

Muintir na gCurach

The Last of the High Kings   d. David Keating, Ben Gibney,
Parallel Films   Suzanne Nicell
                                                        a. David Keating *from the novel by*
                                                        Ferdia MacAnna

RTÉ Independent Productions Unit
commissioned drama:
  – **Bogwoman**   d. & a. Tom Collins
    De Facto Film and Video Productions
  – **Separation Anxiety**   d. Mark Staunton
    Paradox Pictures   a. Shelagh Harcourt
  – **I Went Down**   d. Paddy Breathnach
    Treasure Films/BSÉ   a. Conor McPherson
  – **The Last Bus Home**   d. & a. Johnny Gogan
    Bandit Films
  – **Snakes & Ladders**   d. & a. Trish McAdam
    Livia Film Productions

1997

Glenroe
serial

See page 129.

Fair City
serial

See pages 131–2.

Ros na Rún
Irish language serial

See page 145.

Boys and Men
Finglas/Parallel Film/RTÉ co-production

d. Seán Hinds
a. Brian Lally

81
Mammoth Films production funded by
RTÉ and BSÉ

d. & a. Stephen Burke

Summertime
Storm Productions Ltd funded by
RTÉ and BSÉ

d. Eve Morrison
a. Michael Ennis

Reaper
Temple Films/RTÉ co-production

d. & a. Stephen Bradley

The Bench
Film Base/RTÉ co-production

d. & a. KristenSheridan

Upwardly Mobile
series

See pages 140–1.

Making the Cut
series

d. Martyn Friend
a. John Brown, Eric Deacon
(*based on characters by* Jim Lusby)

Seanchaí
series
A Westway Production for RTÉ and BBCNI
– **An Fear Portaigh** (*The Tall Man*)
– **Cóisir Oíche Shamhna** (*The Hallowe'en Party*)
– **Eadáil** (*The Beachcomber*)
– **An Glantóir** (*The Chimney Sweep*)
– **An Stiléir** (*The Poteen Maker*)

The Budgie
Unicorn Productions

d. & a. Peter Butler

Draíocht
   Crimson Films

d. Aine O'Connor
a. Gabriel Byrne

Debut
   series of new drama on film:
   – Jack's Bicycle
     College of Commerce, Rathmines
   – He Shoots, He Scores
   – Bent Out of Shape
     Roisin Rua Films (Grand Pictures)
   – Out of the Deep Pan
     Initial Film And Television Ltd/BBCNI
   – Alaska
   – Puddy Cat
     BBCNI/Hot Shot Films
   – Masochist
   – Pteranodon
   – Jack
     Little Girl Productions
   – Pips
   – Mercy
   – The Booklover's Tale
     Indi Films
   – Resurrection Man
   – Quickfix
     Vertigo Productions Ltd
   – The Very Stuff
   – Niamh and the Angels
   – The Cake
     BBCNI
   – Prisoners
   – Bovine
     Ruby Films
   – The Thirst
     Line Productions and Sahara Films
   – The Condom
   – BOA
   – Serial Numbers

d. & a. John Moore

d. Damien O'Donnell
d. Orla Walsh

d. Kieron Walsh
a. Tim Loane
d. & a. Michael West
d. Brendan J. Byrne
a. Conor Grimes
d. Fiona Comerford
d. Bill Murphy
d. & a. Mary Mullen

d. Naoise Barry
d. Liam Regan
d. Paul Lenehan

d. Gabriel Levy
d. Eamon Little

d. Lisa Mulcahy
d. John O'Brien
d. Jo Neylin
a. Pat Griffin
d. Ellen Maria Dunleavy
d. & a. Peter McKenna

d. Michael Egan

d. Martin Mahon
d. Barra de Bhaldraithe
d. Jean Pasley

1998

Glenroe
  serial

See page 129.

Fair City   See pages 131–2.
  serial

Ros na Rún   See page 145.
  Irish language serial

Two Lives
  series of plays for television:
  – **Hell for Leather**   *d.* Kieron J. Walsh
                                       a. Roddy Doyle

  – **Golden Wedding**   *a.* Andrea Gibb
  – **Gold in the Streets**   *d.* Elizabeth Gill
    Ferndale Films/Rank Film
    Distribution/RTÉ/BSÉ co-production *a.* Elizabeth Gill,
                                       Noel Pearson, Janet Noble

Soldier's Song   *d.* Kevin Liddy
  Indi Films Production for RTÉ/BSÉ
Pinned   *d. & a.* Ciarán Donnelly
  Parallel Films/RTÉ/BSÉ co-production

Before I Sleep   *d. & a.* Paul Mercier
  Brother Films production for RTÉ/BSÉ

Homeboy   *d.* Mary Mullan
  A Little Girl Films Production for RTÉ/BSÉ

Amongst Women
  serial 4 episodes   *d.* Tom Cairns
  Parallel Films/BBCNI/RTÉ/BSÉ   *a.* Adrian Hodges *adapted from the
                                       novel by* John McGahern

Bolt   *d. & a.* David Caffrey
  Indi Films Production for RTÉ/BSÉ

Racing Homer   *d. & a.* Peter McKenna
  A Ruby Films Production for RTÉ/BSÉ

Basket Full of Wallpaper   *d.* Joe Lee
  Samson Films production for RTÉ/BSÉ *a.* Robert Quinn

My Dinner with Oswald   *d.* Paul Duane
  Blue Light production for RTÉ/BSÉ   *a.* Donal Clarke

Quando   *d. & a.* Declan Recks
  Paradox Pictures production for RTÉ/BSÉ

Falling for a Dancer
  serial 4 episodes   *d.* Richard Standeven
  Parallel Films/BBCNI/RTÉ/BSÉ   *a.* Deirdre Purcell

Kings in Grass Castles
  serial 4 episodes
  Barron Entertainment/RTÉ co-production

Upwardly Mobile   *See page 141.*
  series

The Officer from France   *d.* Tony Barry
                            a. Gary Mitchell

Couched
  Sitcom/Sketch show   *d.* Ferdia MacAnna
                            a. Barry Murphy & Mark Doherty

Most Important   *d.* P. J. Dillon
  Parzival Productions   *a.* P. J. Dillon & David Attoe
Dancing at Lughnasa   *d.* Pat O'Connor
  Ferndale Films   *a.* Frank McGuinness *based on the play*
                              by Brian Friel

Lipservice   *d. & a.* Paul Mercier
  Brother Films

Debut
  series of new drama on film:
    – Freesia of Eden   *d.* Alastair McIlwain
     BBCNI   *a.* Gemma Mullen
    – To the Mountain   *d. & a.* Jean Pasley
    – Let's Pretend   *d. & a.* Grace Joliffe
     Dún Laoghaire Institute of Art,
     Design and Technology
    – Silicon Valerie   *d. & a.* John Simpson
     Black Star Films
    – Getting Close   *d. & a.* Hugh McGory
    – Late   *d.* Vinny Murphy
    – Brood   *d.* Frankie McCafferty
     Parzival Productions   *a.* Ian Kilroy
    – Charming Celia   *d.* David Starkey
     Itchy Feet Film and TV Productions *a.* Michael Burns
    – The Seventh Nocturne   *d. & a.* Felim MacDermot
     Dún Laoghaire Institute of Art,
     Design and Technology

- **Gort na gChamh**
  Straight Feet Productions — *d. & a.* Carol Moore
- **Not Victor** — *d. & a.* Tracy Cullen
- **Jumpers** — *d.* Konrad Jay
  G & H production for BBCNI — *a.* Colin Bateman
- **When the Dust Settles** — *d.* Tom Heaney and Colm McManus
  New Moon Pictures Ltd — *a.* Gail Duncan
- **Another Day** — *d.* Martin Mahon
  The Rocketship Production Company
- **Molly and Me** — *d.* Daire Keogh
  Line Productions and Sahara Films
- **The Last Shout** — *d.* Paul Conway
  Line Productions and Sahara Films
- **The Farmer's Wife** — *d. & a.* Robert Taylor
- **RIB** — *d.* Darren Tiernan
  Monkey House Film Production
- **Retribution in the Year 2050** — *d.* Brendan Muldowney
- **Swag** — *d.* Colm Whelan & Aine Moriarty
- **Flying Saucer Rock and Roll** — *d.* Enda Hughes
  Cousins Pictures — *a.* Enda Hughes & Mike Duffy
- **Stealth** — *d.* Rachel Dowling
- **Zanzibar** — *d.* Chris Roche
  Zanzibar Productions/Pucan Production
- **The Rope Trick** — *d.* Tim Mercier
  — *a.* Hugh Costello
- **Happy Birthday to Me** — *d.* Martin Mahon

RTÉ Independent Productions Unit
commissioned drama:
- **Flesh and Blood**
  Cipango/Metropolitan Films
- **Tales from the Poorhouse** — *d.* Louis Lentin
  series of 4 dramas
  A Crescendo Concept for TnaG and RTÉ: *a.* Eugene McCabe
- **Chrono-Perambulator** — *d.* Damien O'Donnell
  Firesgrove Ltd
- **Land of Spices**
  Samson Films
- **The Big Match**
  Yellow Asylum Films

1999

Glenroe
serial

See page 129.

Fair City
serial

See pages 131–2.

Ros na Rún
Irish language serial

See page 145.

Flesh and Blood
serial 2 episodes
RTÉ/Cipango co-production

d. Robin Davis
a. Natalie Carter

Rainbow's End
An Early Town Films production
funded by RTÉ/BSÉ

d. & a. Alan Archbold

The Breakfast
An Irish Stage and Screen production
funded by RTÉ/BSÉ

d. & a. Peter Sheridan

Chiara
An Indi Films production funded
by RTÉ/BSÉ

d. & a. Chris Roche

Just in Tune
Samson Films/Early Town Films
production funded by RTÉ/BSÉ

d. John Carney & Tom Hall
a. John Carney

Flush
Flushfilms productions
funded by RTÉ/BSÉ

d. Frankie McCafferty
a. Eric Myles

Making Ends Meet
Indi Films for RTÉ/BSÉ

d. Declan Recks
a. Darnien O'Donnell &
Arnold Fanning

Ward Zone
Dún Laoghaire Institute of Art,
Design and Technology/
RTÉ co-production

d. & a. Audrey O'Reilly

Double Calpet
Pegasus Productions for RTÉ/BSÉ

d. & a. Mark Kilroy

Making the Cut
  serial 3 episodes   *d.* Martin Friend *based on characters by* Jim Lusby

Eureka Street   *d.* Adrian Shergold
  Euphoria Films for BBCNI/RTÉ   *a.* Donna Franceschild *adapted from the novel by* Robert McLiam Wilson

DDU   *d.* Alan Grint
  serial   *a.* Michael Russell

Bull Island
  satirical series   *p.* JohnKeogh
            d. Peter McEvoy

Writers/Performers: Elva Crowley, Pearse Lehane, Alan Shortt, Michael Sheridan, Pakie O'Callaghan, Michelle Costello, Frank Twomey.

Ordinary Decent Criminal   *d.* Thaddeus O'Sullivan
  Little Bird/Trigger Street Productions/   *a.* Gerard Stembridge
  Icon Entertainment International

Agnes Browne   *d.* Anjelica Houston
  Hell's Kitchen   *a.* John Goldsmith & Brendan O'Carroll from his book *The Mammy*

Súilin Draíochta
  series dramatised Irish stories   *d. & p.* Gerry McColgan
  Crimson Films for TG4

Debut
  series of new drama on film:
    – **Still Life**   *d. & a.* Michael Hewitt
      Double-Band Films
    – **Garden of Souls**   *d.* Michael Brennan
    – **Lover's Leap**   *d. & a.* Jason Forde
    – **Gun**   *d.* Konrad Jay
    – **Elsewhere**   *d. & a.* Brian Drysdale
    – **Home**   *d. & a.* Collette Cullen
      Igloo Production/Zanzibar Productions
    – **Stranded**   *d.* Ian Fitzgibbon
      Two For The Show (Grand Pictures)   *a.* Brian Fitzgibbon
    – **Fatal Extraction**   *d.* Colin McKeown
      Besom Productions Ltd   *a.* Malachy Harkin
    – **Life on Mars**   *d. & a.* James Cotter
      Dún Laoghaire Institute of Art, Design and Technology

– Green Oranges 　　d. Conor Grimes
　　　　　　　　　　　　a. Eamon Devlin

– They Also Serve　　d. Marin Fulgosi *based on a* Mervyn
　　　　　　　　　　　　Wall *story*

– Solomon I　　　　　d. Colm Whelan
– 7th Heaven　　　　　d. Shimmy Marcus
– Short Life　　　　　d. Imogen Murphy
– The Big Match　　　d. Martin Mahon
– The Good Son　　　d. Seán McGuire
　Fillum Ltd　　　　　a. Stephen MacAnena

RTÉ Independent Productions Unit
commissioned drama:
– Straight to Video　d. Martin Mahon
　series 6 episodes　　a. Darl MacDermott
　Hill 16
– Borstal Boy　　　　d. Peter Sheridan
　Hells Kitchen Ltd　　a. Peter Sheridan & Nye Heron, *based
　　　　　　　　　　　　on the book by* Brendan Behan

– When Brendan Met Trudy　d. Kieran J. Walsh
　Deadly Films 2　　　a. Roddy Doyle
– Nora　　　　　　　d. Pat Murphy
　Volta Films Ltd　　　a. Pat Murphy & Gerard Stembridge
　　　　　　　　　　　　based on the book by Brenda Maddox

– Anytime
　Comet Films

2000

Fair City　　　　　*See pages 131–2.*
　serial

Glenroe　　　　　　*See page 129.*
　serial

Ros na Rún　　　　*See page 145.*
　serial

Bull Island　　　　*See page 152.*
　Satirical series

A Love Divided　　d. Syd McCarthy
　Parallel Films for RTÉ and
　BBC Scotland/BSÉ/　a. Stuart Hepburn
　Arts Council of Northern Ireland

Left Back　　　　　d. Joe McElwaine
　An Egg and Chips production for RTÉ

Dream Kitchen
  A Hit and Run production for RTÉ

d. Barry Dignam
a. Kevin McCarthy

The Case of Majella McGinty
  Rough Magic Film Productions for RTÉ/BSÉ

d. Kirsten Sheridan

a. Morna Regan

Mir Friends
  Esras Film production for RTÉ/BSÉ

d. Peter Kelly
a. John Fagan

Custer's Last Stand-Up
  series RTÉ/BBC co-production

a. Gail Renard, Brian Lynch

In Loving Memory
  RTÉ/BSÉ co-production

d. & a. Audrey O'Reilly

Dogsbody
  Samson Films for RTÉ/BSÉ

d. & a. Karl Golden

Forecourt
  Parallel Films for RTÉ/BSÉ

d. Anne-Marie Casey-O'Connor
a. Katy Hayes

Rebel Heart
  serial 4 episodes
  Palace Pictures production for BBCNI/RTÉ

d. John Strickland

a. Ronan Bennett

Short Cuts
  short film series supported by RTÉ and BSÉ:
  – **Bye Bye Inkhead**
    Liquid Films/Punched Steel Productions
  – **Coolockland**
    Icarus Films
  – **Day One**
    Grand Pictures
  – **Life in the Fast Lane**
    Grand Pictures
  – **The Marriage**
    Hi Ho Productions

d. Adrienne Michel-Long
a. Gai Griffin
d. Brian Tucker
a. Ronan Carr
d. Lisa Mulcahy
a. Margaret Moggan
d. & a. Orla Walsh

d. Darina Gallagher and Kieran McBride
a. Colm Maher

Mystic Knights of Tir na nÓg
  Metropolitan Films/Saban Entertainment/ Sharpmist Limited

d. James Flynn

Oscailt

series of short films funded by TG4 and BSÉ:
- ***Aqua***   *d.* Edel Fitzpatrick
  Macalla Teoranta   *a.* Nina Fitzpatrick
- ***Dillusc***   *d.* Dearbhla Walsh
  Fish Films   *a.* Marina Ní Dhubhain
- ***Deich gCoiscéim***   *d. & a.* Pearse Lehane
  Zanzibar Productions
- ***Filleann an Feall***   *d.* Frankie McCafferty
  Flush Films   *a.* Don Wycherly
- ***Dallacán***   *d.* Cóilín Ó Scolaí
  Twilight Films   *a.* Neil Leyden
- ***Iníon an Fhiaclóra***   *d. & a.* Jacqueline O'Neill
  Zanzibar Films
- ***An Leabhar***   *d.* Robert Quinn
  Rosg Films   *a.* Darach Ó Scolaí
- ***Óstán na gCroíthe Briste***   *d. & a.* Ciaran O'Connor
  Clanvision Films

Debut

series of new drama on film:
- ***Mortice***   *d.* James T. Donnelly
- ***Tale of the Rat That Wrote***   *d.* Billy O'Brien
- ***Dinner at Eight***   *d. & a.* Stephen Moynihan
- ***Underworld***   *d. & a.* Ronan Gallagher
  Pucan Productions
- ***The Long Run***   *d.* Colm McCarthy
  Paradise Pictures
- ***Not a Bad Christmas***   *d.* Enda Walsh
- ***Northern Lights***   *d. & a.* Liam O'Neill
  Paradox Pictures
- ***Half Full, Half Empty***   *d.* Lisa Mulcahy
- ***Choppers***   *d.* Paul Farren
- ***The Great Itch***   *d.* Michael Mahon
  Pucan Productions
- ***Salvage***   *d.* Maeve Murphy
- ***Slumber***   *d.* Emer Reynolds
- ***Blessed Fruit***   *d.* Orla Walsh
  Grand Pictures
- ***Buskers***   *d.* Ian Power
- ***Blind Mice***   *d.* Nick McGinley

   – **Sugar and Spice**   *d.* John McLiduff
   – **Love and Other Unspeakable**   *d.* Brian Fitzgerald
      Orphan Films/Camera Pen Ltd
   – **Clubbing**   *d.* Anthony Byrne
      Indi Films/Igloo Productions
   – **Stainless Steel**   *d.* Colin McIvor
   – **Gravity**   *d.* Romek Delimata
      Zanzibar Productions
   – **Headwrecker**   *d.* Colin McIvor
      Parzival Productions/Three Forks
   – **At Death 's Door**   *d.* Conor Morrissey

RTÉ Independent Productions Unit
commissioned drama:
   – **Paths to Freedom**   *d.* Ian Fitzgibbon
      spoof documentary series   *a.* Ian Fitzgibbon &
      Grand Pictures   Michael McElhatton
   – **Relative Strangers**
      serial 4 episodes   *d.* Giles Foster
      Little Bird/Tatfilm co-production for RTE *a.* Eric Deacon
      financed by FilmstiftungNRW/VVDR/
      Media Programme of the European Union/RTÉ

2001

Glenroe   *See page 129.*
  serial

Fair City   *See pages 131–2.*
  serial

Ros na Rún   *See page 145.*
  serial

Bull Island   *See page 152.*
  satirical series

Black Day at Black Rock   *d. & a.* Gerard Stembridge
  Venus Films production for RTÉ

Beckett on Film
  Blue Angel/Tyrone Productions for RTÉ/
  Channel 4/BSÉ
   – **Waiting for Godot**   *d.* Michael Lindsay-Hogg
   – **What Where**   *d.* Damien O'Donnell

– *Footfalls*   *d.* Walter Asmus
– *Come and Go*   *d.* John Crowley
– *Rockaby*   *d.* Richard Eyre
– *Act without Words I*   *d.* Karel Reisz
– *That Time*   *d.* Charles Garrard
– *Endgame*   *d.* Conor McPherson
– *Play*   *d.* Anthony Minghella
– *Act without Words II*   *d.* Enda Hughes
– *A Piece of Monologue*   *d.* Robin Lefevre
– *Ohio Impromptu*   *d.* Charles Sturridge
– *Rough for Theatre I*   *d.* Kieron J. Walsh
– *Not I*   *d.* Neil Jordan
– *Catastrophe*   ·   *d.* David Mamet
– *Rough for Theatre II*   *d.* Katie Mitchell
– *Breath*   *d.* Damien Hirst
– *Happy Days*   *d.* Patricia Rozema
– *Krapp's Last Tape*   *d.* Atom Egoyan

The Cassidys
  comedy series 6 episodes
  Graph Films for RTÉ

Bachelor's Walk
  series 8 episodes   *d. & a.* John Carney & Tom Hall
  Accomplice Films for RTÉ

On Home Ground
  series 8 episodes   *d.* Ciaran Donnelly, Kevin Liddy,
  Little Bird for RTÉ   Charlie McCarthy, Declan Recks

Debut
  series of new drama on film:
  – *Time*   *d.* Matt Naughton
  – *John Relly Tells All*   *d.* Michael Carolan
  – *The Black Suit*   *d.* Frank Berry
  – *Catch Yourself On*   *d.* Paul Madden
  – *The Church of Acceptance*   *d.* Brendan Muldowney
  – *Escape*   *d.* Stephen Benedict
  – *Smalltalk* Covert Films   *d.* Ronan Burke
  – *Running*   *d.* Anna Rodgers
  – *Mysterious Ways*   *d.* John Simpson
  – *Fatboy and Twintub*   *d.* Clair Breton
  – *Close*   *d.* Ruth Meehan
  – *Guilty of Love*   *d.* Hugh O'Conor

– *The Devil You Know*   d. Colin Bateman
– *Betting the Game*   d. Tanya Reihill
– *The Hall* The Film Factory   d. Doreen O'Connor
– *Swallows*   d. Michael O'Connell
– *Diversion*   d. Josephine Conlon
– *Je Mange l*e Chat*   d. Eoin McGuirk
– *Screenplay*   d. Patrick Butler
– *Taking Pictures*   d. Niamh Nic Roaois
– *Crossed Lines* Covert Films   d. Paul Murphy
– *Man of Few Words*   d. Terence White
– *Odd Sock*   d. Colette Cullen
     Zanzibar Productions

– *The Beauty of Darkness*   d. Kealan O'Rourke
– *To Catch a Crow*   d. Shay Leonard
– *A Walk in the Woods*   d. Adrian Scanlan
– *Freaky Deaky 10 to 1*   d. Anthony Byrne
     Indi Films
– *The Widow's Son*
– *Day One* Grand Pictures   d. Lisa Mulcahy

RTÉ Independent Productions Unit
   commissioned drama:
   – *Random Passage*   d. John N. Smith
     Subotica/CBS   a. Des Walsh *from the novel by* Bernice
                                      Morgan

2002

Fair City   *See pages 131–2.*
   serial

Ros na Rún   *See page 144.*
   serial
No Tears   a. Brian Phelan
   Little Bird and Comet Productions for RTÉ

Fergus's Wedding
   serial 6 episodes   d. Ian Fitzgibbon
   Grand Pictures production for RTÉ   a. Ian Fitzgibbon &
                                      Michael McElhatton

On Home Ground   *See page 157.*
   series

RTÉ Independent Productions Unit commissioned drama:
  – **Saltwater**   *d. & a.* Conor McPherson
    Treasure Films
  – **Home for Christmas**   *d. & a.* Charlie McCarthy

Television drama made by
BBC Northern Ireland, 1989–2002

1989

Beyond the Pale	*d.* Diarmuid Lawrence
	a. William Trevor
Chinese Whispers	*d.* Stuart Burge
	a. Maurice Leitch
Monkeys	*d.* Danny Boyle
	a. Paul Muldoon
The Hen House	*d.* Danny Boyle
	a. Frank McGuinness
Elephant	*d. & a.* Alan Clarke
The Nightwatch	*d.* Danny Boyle
	a. Ray Brennan

1990

The Englishman's Wife	*d.* Robert Cooper
	a. Holly Chandler
A Safe House	*d.* Moira Armstrong
	a. Bill Morrison
August Saturday	*d.* Diarmuid Lawrence
	a. William Trevor

1991

Arise and Go Now	*d.* Danny Boyle
	a. Owen O'Neill

Children of the North	*a.* based on novels by M. S. Power
Murder in Eden	*d.* Nicholas Renton
3-part serial	*a.* Shane Connaughton
Burlington Films for BBCNI	

1992

Force of Duty	*d.* Pat O'Connor
BBCNI in association with RTÉ	*a.* Bill Morrison and Chris Ryder

1993

Love Lies Bleeding	*d.* Michael Winterbottom
	a. Ronan Bennett

1994

A Breed of Heroes	*d.* Diarmuid Lawrence
	a. Charles Wood *based on the novel by* Alan Judd
All Things Bright and Beautiful	*d. & a.* Barry Devlin
Hilltown Ltd/Good Film Company for BBCNI in association with BSÉ	

1995

The Hanging Gale	*d.* Diarmuid Lawrence
4-part serial	*a.* Allan Cubitt
Little Bird for BBCNI in association with RTÉ	
Life after Life	*d.* Tim Fywell
	a. Graham Reid
Runway One	*d.* David Drury
2-part serial	*a.* Barry Devlin
Burlington Films	

1996

Ballykissangel
   series 1 to 6   *1996–2001*
Ballykea Production for World Productions for BBC Northern Ireland
   series 1
writers: Kieran Prendiville, John Forte.
directors: Richard Standeven, Paul Harrison.

The Precious Blood   *d.* John Woods
                                                 a. Graham Reid

Safe and Sound   *d.* Tim Prager
   series   *a.* Baz Taylor & Bill Pryde
   Pearson Television

Loving   *d.* Diarmuid Lawrence
   Samson Films/Green Films   *a.* Maggie Wadey *based on the novel by*
                                                    Henry Green

The Van   *d.* Stephen Frears
   Deadly Films/BBC Films/Fox Searchlight a. Roddy Doyle

A Man of No Importance   *d.* Suri Krishnamma
   BBC Films/Little Bird/Majestic Films   *a.* Barry Devlin

Northern Lights
   series of short films:
   – Skintight   *d. & a.* John Forte
      First City Feature for BBCNI
   – The Cake   *d.* Jo Neylin
      Fena Films/Indica Films for BBCNI   *a.* Pat Griffin
      and Northern Ireland Film Council
   – Everybody's Gone   *d.* N. G. Bristow
      De Facto Films for BBCNI and the   *a.* Martin Meenan
      NI Film Commission
   – Out of the Deep Pan   *d.* Kieran J. Walsh
      BBC in association with Initial Film   *a.* Tim Loane
      and Television Ltd
   – Dance Lexie Dance   *d.* Tim Loane
      Raw Nerve for BBCNI   *a.* Dave Duggan
   – Puddy Cat   *d.* Brendan J. Byrne
      Hot Shot Films for BBCNI   *a.* Conor Grimes

1997

Ballykissangel
   series 2
   writers: Kieran Prendiville, John Forte, Niall Leonard, Jo O'Keefe, Rio Fanning
   directors: Paul Harrison, Dermot Boyd.

Northern Lights *series of short films*
   – The Long Walk   *d.* Kieran McGuigan
      About-Face for BBCNI   *a.* Gerard O'Hare

– Jumpers	*d.* Konrad Jay
G&H Production for BBCNI	*a.* Colin Bateman
– The Freesia of Eden	*d.* Alistair McIlwain
Footage for BBCNI and ACN1	*a.* Gemma McMullan

1998

Ballykissangel
   series 3
writers: Kieran Prendiville, Barry Devlin, Tim Loane, Rio Fanning, Niall Leonard, Felicity Hayes-McCoy, Robert Jones' Ted Gannon.
directors: Dermot Boyd, Tom Cotter, Paul Harrison.

Give My Head Peace
comedy series	*d.* Stephen Butcher
	a. Michael McDowell,
	Tim McGarry, Damon Quinn

The Ambassador
   series
   Ecosse Films/Irish Screen/BBCNI
   series 1
writers: Russel Lewis, Tim Prager, Chris Russell, Julian Jones.
directors: Patrick Lau, Ken Grieve, Syd McCartney.

Falling for a Dancer
4-part serial	*d.* Richard Standeven
Parallel Films Production for BBCNI	*a.* Deirdre Purcell
in association with RTÉ	

Amongst Women
4-part serial	*d.* Tom Cairns
Parallel Films for BBCNI in association	*a.* Adrian Hodges *based on the novel*
with RTÉ and BSÉ	*by* John McGahern

Divorcing Jack
BBC Films/Winchester Films/Scala	*d.* David Caffrey
	a. Colin Bateman

Northern Lights
   series of short films
– Dah Dit Dah	*d. & a.* N. G. Bristow
Tall Stories for BFI and BBCNI	

1999

Ballykissangel
  series 4
writers: Robert Jones, Mark Holloway, Ted Gannon, Jimmy Murphy, Barry Devlin, Stephen Plaice.
directors: Simon Meyers, N. G. Bristow, Simon Massey, Mike Cocker, Peter Lydon.

The Ambassador
  series 2
writers: Julian Jones, Tim Prager, Neil McKay, Hugh Costello.
directors: Matthew Evans, Crispin Reece, A. J. Quinn.

Eureka Street
  4-part serial
  Euphoria Films production for BBCNI in association with RTÉ

d. Adrian Shergold
a. Donna Franceschild
based on the novel by Robert McLiam Wilson

A Rap at the Door

d. Suri Krishnamma
a. Barry Devlin

Vicious Circle
  BBCNI/Irish Screen

d. David Blair
a. Kieran Prendiville

Northern Lights *series of short films*
  – Fatal Extraction
  Besom Productions for BBCNI

d. Colin McKeown
a. Malachy Martin

2000

Ballykissangel
  series 5
writers: Ted Gannon, Mark Holloway, Terry Hodgkinson, Declan Croghan, Paul Coates, Mick Martin, Stuart Blackburn.
directors: Simon Massey, Peter Lydon, Mike Cocker, Paul Duane.

McCready and Daughter (*pilot*)
  Ecosse films for BBCNI
Rebel Heart
  4-part serial
  Picture Palace Production for BBCNI in association with Irish Screen, RTÉ, BSÉ and October Productions Ltd

d. A. J. Quinn
a. Robert Jones
d. John Strickland
a. Ronan Bennett

Wild about Harry   *d.* Declan Lowney
   BBC Films/Scala/MBP in association   *a.* Colin Bateman
   Wave Pictures and Winchester Films

2001

Ballykissangel
   series 6
writers: Kieran Prendiville, John Flanagan, Andy McCullough, Ursula Aspill-
de Brun.
directors: Paul Harrison, Frank Smith, Alan McMillan.

Nice Guy Eddie *(pilot)*   *d.* Douglas McKinnon
                                                          a. Johanne McAndrew and
                                                             Elliot Hope

McCready and Daughter *series*   *d.* David Innes Edwards,
   Ecosse Films for BBCN1   Piers Haggard, Dermot Boyd
                                                          a. Ted Gannon, Robert Jones,
                                                             John Flanagan, Andy McCulloch,
                                                             John Martin Johnson

2002

Nice Guy Eddie   *d.* Douglas McKinnon, Alan
   series   McMillan, Morag McKinnon
                                                          a. Johanne McAndrew, Steve
                                                             Lawson

As the Beast Sleeps   *d.* Harry Bradbeer
                                                          a. Gary Mitchell

Index